for my friends. ~~~~~~~~~~~~

With the Author's best wishes.

A DIVERSITY OF BIRDS

a personal journey of discovery

by

GEORGE STEBBING-ALLEN

[signature]

THE UMBERLEIGH PRESS

Published by   THE UMBERLEIGH PRESS, DEVON
                    Sales: PO Box 41, Bangor, Gwynedd LL57 1SB, G.B.

Typeset by   CELTIC TYPESETTERS & PRINTERS
                    Rainbow Business Centre, Swansea Enterprise Park
                    Llansamlet, Swansea SA7 9EH

Printed by   HENRY LING LTD., THE DORSET PRESS
                    Dorchester, Hants.

ISBN   1 85944 000 2

A CIP catalogue record for this book is available from the British Library.

Cover Illustration The Red-billed streamertail from an original
                    watercolour by MARTIN WOODCOCK.

Original line-drawings by STEPHEN LINGS.

Maps and artwork by David White of Creative Associates, Oxford.

A
Diversity of Birds

a personal journey of discovery . . .

This book is Dedicated with Gratitude and Affection to
DAVID WEBSTER
Engineer, Industrialist, Ornithologist, Friend
without whose encouragement it could not have been written

"What motivated the author? ...
More than a dash of egotism, an
easy seduction by Nature's sensuali-
ty, some anti-rationalist obstinacy,
the positive enjoyment of difficult
endeavours, and the tawdry taste for
adventures, preferably outdoors.
Above all, the intoxication of learn-
ing about life directly through the
gut, of rediscovering Nature as fresh
and palpable on every field-trip."

Jonathan Evan Maslow
"Bird of Life, Bird of Death."

CONTENTS

TABLE OF CONTENTS

ACKNOWLEDGEMENTS

In 1991, when I first started looking for a book to answer the "why?" questions that I was then beginning to ask, I sought opinions from a variety of people to see if such a book did in fact exist. I wonder to what extent they realize that *A Diversity of Birds* is a direct response to their unanimous belief that it didn't. I am particularly grateful for this response from Sir David Attenborough; Ian Dawson, the RSPB librarian, who suggested details of source material; and Peter Exley, the Catalogue Editor of the Natural History Book Service.

Special thanks are due to my friend, Richard T Holmes, the Harris Professor of Environmental Biology at Dartmouth College, Hanover, New Hampshire, USA. His encouraging correspondence contains the following seminal passage —

The exercise of posing the questions, providing answers where possible or perhaps of pointing out what it would take to come up with an answer, is commendable and should be stimulating to 'intelligent laypeople' if not also to many scientists. Also, just the emphasis on encouraging people to be inquisitive about what they are seeing is excellent.

Though he is perhaps unaware of his contribution, Professor Ghillean Prance, Director of the Royal Botanic Gardens, Kew, had more of an influence than he knows on my approach to the subject. I thank him warmly for his suggestion, voiced in a *Daily Telegraph* interview, that scientists can best improve their public image by spending time interpreting their work to the layman in understandable terms.

However, one person responded to my enquiry by saying *"I don't know of any such book; why don't you write one?"* This was Mike Parr, until recently a member of the BirdLife International secretariat. To him I owe the stimulus to start writing the book in the first place, and a corresponding debt of gratitude.

Whilst it is possible for the seed of an idea to originate in the mind of a single person, that seed will only grow and sprout in the fertile humus of conversations and discussions with well-informed people, in a process akin to that whereby novice birdwatchers seek the company of those more knowledgeable than themselves.

Over the years, it has been my good fortune to watch birds with very many such people, and to discuss all manner of ornithological subjects with them. To them all I extend my thanks for their unwitting but invaluable contributions to *A Diversity of Birds*. I hope they will not view an alphabetical listing as too impersonal a vehicle for my thanks.

I therefore thank — Jaime Alvarado, Sheila Alliez, Peter Aspinall, Bert Axell, the late Dick Bagnall-Oakley, Jill Bale, Leo Batten, Brian Bell, the late

Billy Bishop, Bryan Bland, Arthur Brown, Chris Bullock, Joe Caravella, Stuart Chambers, Jean-Pierre Choisy, John Ciaffone, the late Peter Conder, David Crockett, Gary Diller, Ted Dintersmith, Bryan Donegan, Sally Douglas, Philippe Dubois, Claude Edwards, John Emsley, John Fanshawe, David Fisher, Dave and Carole Foote, Ray Galea, Henry Genthe, John Gooders, Georgina Green, Richard Grimmett, Trevor Gunton, Richard Homan, Richard Howard, Bob Howl, S A Hussein, Jim Ireland, Greg and Debi Jackson, Sue and Olav Johnsen, Goran Karlsson, Peter Kelton-Groves, Ben King, Helen Kittinger, Tony Long, Sandy Macfarlane, Peter Martin, Richard May, Zoe McLaughlin, Richard and Margot Merrick, Mary Muller, Angus Murray, Dan Muteanu, Folkert Nieuwland, Peter Partington, Deedee Petro, Peter Rathbone, Ian Reid, Par Sandberg, Jeremy Sorensen, Phoebe Snetsinger, Joe Sultana, Ann and Robert Sutton, Rowley Taylor, Wim Vader, Monika Webster, David Yekutiel and Denis Yong. The list is long, as befits the length of time covered; and my thanks are deep and heartfelt for good companionship and ornithological help. If there are any omissions from the list the fault is mine alone.

Invidious as it may be, I have to single out three people for special thanks; Bryan Donegan, birding friend of 20 years standing, and Angus Murray, doyen of the Buckinghamshire Bird Club, for offering comments and advice on passages as they emerged; and Peter Rathbone, until recently Clwyd County Recorder, for checking the whole manuscript for ornithological accuracy.

My objective in *A Diversity of Birds* has been a synthesis of the technical literature for the benefit of the lay reader. This, of course, has entailed a large amount of research ; and I am endebted to two librarians in particular for their cheerful assistance — Effie Warr of the British Museum (Natural History) at Tring, and Dorothy Haig of the Department of Earth Sciences at Oxford University.

My two artists deserve, and have earned, my special gratitude. Their skill, craftsmanship and sensitivity speak through every part of their work. Martin Woodcock knows Jamaica and has stayed at the Great House with Arthur and Robert Sutton; and by painting the Red-billed streamertail from the heart has immeasurably advanced the cause of Jamaican conservation. Stephen Lings is rare amongst artists for his instinctive iterpretation of my concepts; and for his wide knowledge that ensured that when I asked for a Fluttering shearwater that is precisely what I got. His line drawings highlight significant events and emotions along my journey of discovery; but his skill has ensured that the memories that they encapsulate are sealed in a way that words alone cannot express.

Finally, my thanks must go to Judith Loades of the Umberleigh Press. Her commitment to *A Diversity of Birds* was immediate, and her support throughout has been both enthusiastic and total.

FOREWORD

A Diversity of Birds" is both a captivating and stimulating book, and sets the reader thinking, as well as longing for the opportunity of visiting the ends of the Earth.

The Author describes how he became aware of world biodiversity by the study of birds and — in awe — realized the scientific, moral and ethical necessity of both protecting and respecting this remarkable, improbable and delectable phenomenon. He indicates the need for studying the questions of change that stem from the passage of evolutionary and geological time; and that the best way to begin this education is to be come a birdwatcher — not just a twitcher — and thus to reach a fundamental understanding of distribution and associated diversity.

George Stebbing-Allen illustrates how the hobby becomes first a voyage of discovery and then of dedication to the encouragement of worldwide bird protection. It is a beautiful peg on which to hang the conservation of the habitat and its associated fauna and flora.

This book, however, is not merely another cry for protection. The delight in, and love of birds seeps through between every line; and it is this enthusiasm coupled with experience in the field which proves infectious. As I turned the pages I suddenly found myself wondering what possessed me to specialize in the study of fleas rather than birds.

Ashton Wold
Peterborough
December 1993   MIRIAM ROTHSCHILD

v

PROLOGUE

The Market for Birdwatching.

Rutland is a county in the English midland shires which, until it was absorbed into Leicestershire by the 1974 boundary changes, enjoyed independent status of long historical standing. In 1975 a vast low lying area between Oakham and Empingham was flooded to create Rutland Water, a reservoir that enjoys fame as one of Europe's largest man-made lakes. Since its construction it has become one of the most important wildfowl sanctuaries in Britain, especially during winter and passage periods; and as it attracts birds so it also attracts those who watch birds. Nine miles of shoreline along the western arms have become a nature reserve covering 350 acres.

In recent years, and as a measure of both the commercial and community aspects of birdwatching, the British Birdwatching Fair has become established at this nature reserve as the premier event of its kind. In 1991 I went to the Fair, and on a lovely summer day it was very well attended by people from all over the country.

Many aspects of the Fair made an impact on me. For a start, I was impressed by the huge country-wide constituency for bird-watching and bird-related activities. It is on record that over the last 20 years or so the RSPB has increased its member-ship at least tenfold, and this is some measure of the size of the birding community; but not until I saw the overflowing car park at Rutland Water did I fully appreciate the sheer weight of numbers. This is of even greater significance in that there are many birdwatchers who are not members of the RSPB.

No trader at these events exhibits for fun. They all do so with a reasonable expectation of immediate or at least future business, and it was clear to me that the majority of the exhibitors were satisfied with their levels of business. So, the second feature that impressed me was the amount of money being spent or being committed for future spending.

Spending on what is for most of us a hobby must come from disposable income, that which is left over after the essentials of life-food, housing, clothing, heating — have been paid for. In 1991 the United Kingdom was in the grip of a fearsome recession; if there was enough disposable income around at that time to warrant holding a Bird Fair in the first place, it can only mean that the birding constituency take their birding very seriously indeed. It also means, as many have long suspected, that such a hobby is governed more by the heart than by the head; and may actually flourish in a recession as an antidote to pessimism.

I quickly realized that there was much to learn from understanding what items were attracting this purchasing power, and it took me no time at all to list three major areas: 1. optical equipment, 2. books and 3. overseas birding holidays. Optical equipment is, of course, the essential prerequisite for this hobby; but the significance of the other two spending areas needed more clarification.

In common with very many people and most birdwatchers I love books and have done so all my life; but I was intrigued in this context to view books and foreign birding holidays in juxtaposition. The typical birding bookshop represented at the Bird Fair carried a wide selection of stock ranging, for example, from *The birds of Oxfordshire* to *Phylogeny and Classification of Birds — a Study in Molecular Evolution*. Yet it seemed to me that there was a preponderance of books with such titles as *A Guide to the Birds of Thailand* or *Top Birding Spots in Southern Africa* — the *where to go and what to see* category that is the essential link between books and foreign birdwatching holidays.

Having myself watched birds in a number of foreign countries and knowing my own motivations, I pursued my investigations in an attempt to understand the motivations of the shoppers at the Bird Fair. Did they, I wondered, have any greater motivation than merely to add ever more species to their life lists, or to satisfy at one and the same time both their collector's instinct and their wanderlust? Or did they genuinely and with some degree of frustration seek to increase their knowledge of worldwide avian distribution and diversity?

Of course, the birders at the Fair come from all levels of experience and involvement, from the "just starting" (or even the "not quite started") right up to the University ornithologist and the busily lobbying pressure group Chairman. Equally obvious, is the preponderance of interested amateurs, but birdwatching is a study where amateurs and professionals alike are continually learning their craft. Moreover, amateurs usually suffer from other commitments that deny them the luxury of studying their craft in the depth that they might prefer.

In the weeks and months that followed the Bird Fair I gradually came to a conclusion, inspired by this juxtaposition of bird books and overseas birdwatching holidays. Here it is.

Birdwatchers in ever-increasing numbers are travelling the world to watch birds in unfamiliar countries. In books they read which birds are available in which countries, and from field guides learn the taxonomy and identification criteria of their chosen regional avifauna. But from the books that are accessible to them in their limited time, they do not appear able to learn very easily the reason why birds occur where they do.

I have often been surprised how easily birdwatchers seem able merely to accept that groupings of birds are the way they are, and that even a process so fundamental to diversification as adaptive radiation is so poorly understood. Maybe a lack of time is more critical than a lack of interest,

2

yet to view the tits on the British list outside the context of adaptive radiation makes the understanding of tanagers and hummingbirds so much more difficult.

Furthermore, I came to believe that many birdwatchers consider the why questions to be actually less important that the what and the where questions. A number of clubs exist to promote the study of and interest in various faunal regions of the world; yet their studies and pronouncements in the main are inward-looking, and appear to take little account of why a regional avifauna is unique in the way that attracted them to it in the first place. There may well be a knock-on effect that restricts membership.

It is a moot point whether this is a source of frustration or inconvenience to the main body of travelling birdwatchers; but it seems to me that a proper study of birds is incomplete without the why answers alongside the what and the where answers. And from my investigations I failed to locate a book that answers the why questions in a manner generally accessible to busy but interested amateur birdwatchers. This book therefore aims to fill the gap.

Right at the outset the reader may like to know the philosophical rationale behind the presentation of material in the particular form that I have chosen.

Summary of the Book.

My fundamental view of subjects as complex as ornithology and bird-watching is in fact quite simply stated. I view ornithology as a science in which a wide variety of objective data are studied and from which conclusions are drawn. In these ways it is no different from any other scientific discipline, and possesses normal professional ethics and protocol. By contrast, bird-watching, though closely related to ornithology, is essentially an amateur pursuit; and because to its devotees its pursuit is more of an end in itself than a means to an end, it is more likely to elicit from them a more personal, more emotional response.

The structure of the book reflects this fundamental view, and accepts that most birdwatchers who take their hobby seriously will be led to the more objective and scientific aspects of ornithology. The book is therefore essentially a sandwich. The meat in the filling is scientific; the top slice of bread is the process that led me to the hobby and from there to the science; and the bottom slice is a glorification of that science around the world, from my obviously personal perspective.

Part I traces how my antecedents led me to ornithology and the joy of birds. Initially learning my trade in the UK, I quickly acquired a preference for birdwatching by habitat and season — and, yes, by diversity — rather than the more frenetic and less focussed activities of the twitcher, a term that I shall define in due course. As my horizons widened with my increasing travels, I came to appreciate ever wider aspects of ornithology and conservation, in particular eco-tourism, international bird protection and geographical diversity. Being naturally inquisitive I soon started asking questions.

These questions lead me naturally and logically into Part II, and this has to be scientific. In the context I treasure a quotation by Professor Ghillean Prance, Director of the Royal Botanic Gardens at Kew, and winner in 1993 of the prestigeous International Cosmos Prize for his work towards conservation, especially in the the Amazonian rain forest. Asked in an newspaper interview to state one way in which scientists could best improve their public image, he replied *"Be prepared to spend some time interpreting their work to the layman in understandable terms"*(my italics). Every visitor to Kew Gardens knows that Professor Prance lives out his vision in the clarity of botanical presentation at every flower bed, hothouse and exhibition area. Would that all scientists were as honest and accessible.

In attempting to answer the questions concerning the distribution and diversity of birds, and the phenomenon of endemism that is, after all, merely a part of each, I have inevitably to enter the realms of science — geology, biogeography, and biology, both the evolutionary and the environmental. My printed sources are all available to those with the time and the inclination to spend long hours in libraries, but in my experience the majority of amateur birdwatchers prefer to spend long hours in the field watching birds. Thus I follow Prof Prance's advice, if at one remove, by interpreting the arcana of our trade in terms understandable to lay birdwatchers.

I show how a study of geology interprets the forces that have shaped the world as we know it today, and demonstrate the link between the theory of Continental Drift and present day avian distribution. As an example, I use the break-up of the ancient super-continent of Gondwanaland and its subsequent modification by volcanoes and the uplift of mountain ranges to demonstrate the physical causes of evolutionary change. As a further example I take a novel standpoint to view two seminally interesting areas — Indonesia and the Central American landbridge — to show how these processes continue to this day even though the slowness of geological time prevents anything more personal than a theoretical awareness.

With more than a passing nod in the direction of Charles Darwin, I view aspects of his theories of natural selection and the survival of the fittest in the light of recent trends in evolutionary biological thought, in particular the concept of contingency popularized by Stephen Jay Gould; species adapting to survive respond to unique circumstances, with no guarantee that such a situation could ever be replicated if the so-called "tape of life" were to be re-run. The implications for avian diversity are startling, as they are for every form of life, ourselves included. Maybe they are not often enough considered by those birdwatchers who view the evolutionary effects of climatic and other environmental factors solely from a contemporary position.

Part III is gloriously and unashamedly an anthology of great bird-watching experiences. These can be enjoyed vicariously by armchair birdwatchers, or used as bait for the more adventurous. I justify this approach — if justification be needed — as a contrast to the academic and theoretical matters considered in Part II. What, after all, is the point of knowing that the Resplendent quetzal, jewel in the crown of Neotropical diversity, is endemic in two races to Central America, if you do not follow this up by marvelling in person at this luscious trogon in its moist Costa Rican cloud forests? Head and heart, scientific ornithology and emotional birdwatching. What other combination could possibly give greater pleasure?

Experiencing Joy in Birdwatching.

I may or may not be a typical ornithologist, but it is from my own experiences and my own studies that this book is written. I can approach my task in no other way than to use as a model my own circumstances and background — genetic and conditioned — my learning processes, my travel and study opportunities and my ornithological predilections. To read what I write on such ornithological matters as distribution, diversity and endemism, it will help readers to know by which routes I come to hold such opinions, and by whose authority I hold them.

During the course of my personal journey of discovery and alongside the efforts I have made to chart the progress of my ornithological development, readers may like to compare their own situations, opinions and knowledge with mine; but just as there are many routes to the one goal of true and proper understanding, I do not expect everyone to have followed the same route as me or to agree with all my conclusions.

It has been said that any science with more than seven variables is an art, and by that criterion it is debatable whether bird-watching is an art or a science. Parallel to my study of scientific ornithology, I have myself experienced many emotions in the course of my birdwatching — awe, wonder, disbelief, frustration, hope, exhilaration, anger.

My personal philosophy of life, and one that guarantees much health and cheerfulness of spirits, can be summed up not by the pursuit of happiness but by the discovery of joy. Joy is the one over-riding emotion that remains when all else departs, and is the one without which both bird-

5

watching and ornithology lose their vital spark. Joy from the heart. Joy at discovery, joy at re-discovery, joy at the unexpected, joy at understanding, joy at accepting the unknowable, joy at beauty, joy at power, joy for the sake of joy itself; but most of all, joy that birds exist at all — for our study and our interest, and most of all for our delight.

PART I

A LEGACY OF BUTTERFLIES

CHAPTER 1

IN THE BEGINNING;
A BREATH OF FRESH AIR

There must be a beginning, but where and how? Some absorbing passions are handed on from one generation to the next, like music or skilled craftsmanship. Some are more passively absorbed under the influence of teachers and mentors; a passionate interest in the Classics or in Physics, for example, is most likely to be inculcated by a charismatic and dedicated teacher. Young people respond best when exposed to widely varying experiences and stimuli, yet it is unusual for the interests they adopt to be utterly divorced from nature and nurture. I am sure that genes play their part here, as elsewhere. As we may look like our parents or grandparents, so we may - quite naturally - follow their interests. So it was with me.

To understand how this came about, we must go back to the 1870s when Professor John Tyndall, FRS, one of the first men to climb the Matterhorn, analysed the air at Hindhead on the hills of the Surrey/Hampshire border. He published the results which showed that the purity of the Hindhead air matched that of the Swiss Alps, and backed his findings by buying land in the area on which to build a home. Coupled to the recently opened London and South-western Railway line that ran from London to Portsmouth via Haslemere, this episode made the whole area around Hindhead and Haslemere immensely attractive to those suffering from the pollution of London with its attendant fogs and tuberculosis.

For a start, Alfred (later Lord) Tennyson had built his Aldworth retreat in 1866 across the valley from Hindhead on the Blackdown hills. The unspoilt pine-clad hills were equally irresistible to those who were well-off and who, in particular, may have had a member of the family suffering from tuberculosis. Moreover, they attracted professional people who were obliged to be frequently in London but who much preferred not to live there. Two such people were to have an immense influence on the area; Mr (later Sir) Jonathan Hutchinson, an emminent surgeon, and Sir Robert Hunter, a senior civil servant, better known to posterity for other reasons. Over the years, their large and cultured families contributed enormously to the artistic, theatrical and scientific life of Haslemere.

Of the cultural elements of our life today, two had their origin in the Haslemere of that time. That same Sir Robert Hunter was a founding father of the National Trust, the body which, amongst other things, protects the pine-clad hills of Hindhead where this whole sequence began. Arnold Dolmetsch, the musicologist, moved to Jesse's in 1917. From this can be traced the revival of interest in Rennaissance and Baroque music and its playing on original or authentically copied instruments. Now, in the 1990s, there is a general acceptance by many musicians that period music is best played on period instruments; and the Haslemere Music

Festival, inaugurated by Arnold Dolmetsch in 1925, is still a persuasive vehicle for these ideas.

Haslemere also attracted Frank Oldaker, a schoolmaster in his early 30s, who moved there in 1904 with his wife Annie and their two small children. Frank, however, found more than just the good fresh air of Haslemere to his liking. His passion was the Lepidoptera - butterflies and moths. He studied them, he bred them, he collected them, he wrote about them, he loved them.

When he arrived in Haslemere he found the Haslemere Natural History Society. This had been founded in 1888 by a certain Colonel William Mason and energetically supported in its early days by Sir Jonathan Hutchinson and Sir Robert Hunter. Frank joined immediately. As early as 1906 he was its secretary when the Society settled into its new headquarters at the Educational Museum; and for the year 1933/4 he was its President. For fifty years he led an annual entomological ramble, never wavering even through two world wars; and through his enthusiasm and generous encouragement of the young, he ensured that his love of the Lepidoptera would extend far beyond his own lifetime. Frank's legacy of butterflies continues to this day. Should you wish to join a butterfly ramble in and around the small Sussex village of Chailey, now in the 1990s, it is likely that your leader will be Jenny Barbour, Frank's granddaughter and my first cousin. The lineage is complete and is running true.

Frank was an approximate contemporary of Walter Lord Rothschild, scion of a family world famous for collecting - from fine wine to hummingbirds and from Sevres porcelaine to butterflies. Walter Rothschild was doing on a larger scale at his museum at Tring what Frank was doing in Haslemere. Remember, this was still the heyday of the Victorian and post-Victorian Collector; but lest we, with our contemporary perspective and the benefit of hindsight, decry the habit, let us by way of example consider the value to science of museum bird skins, and the criteria for determining ornithological type specimens.

Collections, then, play an important part in the science of taxonomy, as Walter Rothschild was to prove. Through his many collectors and his Curator of Lepidoptera, Dr Karl Jordan, he established the principle of what might be called "macro collecting." By comparing the maximum number of specimens of a single species, he established that it is possible to see laid out in the cabinet those minute and clinal variations that indicate full and sub-speciation.

And in Frank Oldaker's cabinet drawers there appeared his own version of Walter Rothschild's macro collection, each specimen and variation meticulously labelled. On his death in 1956 his foreign collection

8

was bequeathed to the British Museum (Natural History), with his British collection destined for Oxford's Hope Institute; both institutions ensuring his work for posterity.

Those who lived through this period in Haslemere recall it with nostalgia as something approaching a Golden Age; and into this amazing environment, where the flames of cultural and scientific enquiry burnt so brightly, was my mother, Lois, born in 1909. Since she was the youngest of Frank and Annie's children, it is hardly surprising that she saw more of them in her early years, than did her brother and sister. In this way, she unwittingly received more of their attention and influence. Gradually, and no doubt genetically, by living an open air life in an interesting countryside, and - I suspect - by accompanying Frank on his butterfly rambles, she came herself to develop an interest in Natural History. But why was it, I wonder, that she chose to concentrate on flowers? (This is a pattern that I have subsequently seen repeated, in my friends Arthur Sutton and his son Robert in Jamaica. It intensifies the very particular interest I have knowing why, in a second generation, the precise focus of natural history interest should change from the first.)

Lois was something of an artist, and in her youth decorated her botany notebooks most beautifully. In later life the works of Marjorie Blamey and W Keble Martin were to give her much vicarious pleasure.

Thus it follows, as night follows day, that I didn't stand a chance. Being my mother's son and my grandfather's grandson, I was bound by nature as well as nurture to adopt an interest in natural history. I have shared orchid rambles with Lois, and - in my youth - butterfly rambles with Frank. Yet, true to the same genetic quirk that diverted Lois from butterflies to flowers, it was to birds that I turned when my interest in natural history was eventually awakened.

I have four, and only four, ornithological memories of my childhood. Great crested grebes on the lake at Wisley, Red-backed shrikes on Ashstead Common, Nightingales on Ranmore Common, and a Redstart in our own suburban garden at Kew - all Surrey locations, and none so far from Haslemere as to loose the connection.

But cricket, politics and an early interest in travel were all to intervene before I turned to natural history.

Those who absorb an interest by osmosis over a period from a teacher or other mentor will find that interest creeping up on them, till they take it for granted and cannot remember a time when it wasn't there. Others, in the manner of St Paul, have a blinding conversion, a watershed when that which follows is totally unlike anything that went before. This was my way.

In May 1968 I found myself at an emotional crossroads. It was the point when I ditched my superficial interests in favour of those that were deep and, I now know, inherited; when I threw overboard the interests imposed by transitory social pressures and allowed the real me to surface. In retrospect, I know that the deep and abiding passion for birds was there all along, just needing a catalyst to bring it out; a seed lying dormant in the desert awaiting the downpour to make it sprout.

On Spring Bank Holiday Monday I was taken to Weirwood Reservoir near the Ashdown Forest in Sussex. My wise old friend just happened to have a spare pair of binoculars at the very moment we needed them to watch a pair of Great crested grebes displaying. Those birds again! Unlike the earlier Wisley experience, these charismatic birds were now ready to be my catalyst. The time was right, the circumstances were right, and my true nature came charging to the surface. In the best traditions of Frank and Lois, I was a student of Natural History. But gloriously and independently I had chosen a different discipline - I was an Ornithologist.

CHAPTER 2

*A CHANCE ENCOUNTER WITH
A DUSKY WARBLER*

Some changes in birdwatching since 1968.

As I start to write about birdwatching in the 1990s, I find it something of an effort to remember how very different it was when I started in 1968. Certainly, one measure is to compare membership of the RSPB — though it by no means compares the whole picture. When I joined in 1968 the membership was less than 70,000, and birdwatching was still some way short of the mass participation activity that it is today. Membership is now (November 1993) in excess of 870,000.

In some ways, particularly in quality, birdwatching has changed for the better over the intervening years; for the respected science of ornithology remains a science and is still respected; now supported by a larger field force of better informed observers, ranging from those who minutely observe common birds or well defined local patches, to others who specialize in monitoring and recording the incidence of rarities and vagrants. As with any fast-growing activity, some participants are bound to be less dedicated than others; but it is rare, if not unheard of, to find birdwatchers at any level who are not prepared to increase their knowledge.

The forces that have brought about the changes in birdwatching over the last quarter century are many and varied; and if in considering some of them I omit those which other people consider important, I defend my actions by choosing those which seem significant to me. The invention of twitching and its explosion in popularity I consider to be the most significant of all, and therefore deal with it under its own heading. Let me start by considering some other forces which I categorize as Social, Marketing and Technological.

Social.

The increase in both leisure time and disposable income have materially affected our response to birdwatching. We now have the time and the mobility with which to explore further afield, both being underpinned by the greater financial confidence bequeathed by the 1980s. (Anyone still unconvinced that bird-watching thrives in a recession should re-read my Prologue; and psychologists might even conclude that birdwatching actually flourishes more in a recession as an antidote to pessimism.)

Social pressures in the community put pressure on the housing market; whilst a greater demand for office space and industrial units flows as another legacy of the 1980s, in terms of an increased entreprenurial spirit powered by an increase in redundancies. If you wish to seek evidence for this contention, look no further than the recent expansion of the Poole conurbation and the conservation pressures that this has placed on the fragile Dorset heath habitat. A natural resource such as this increases in importance — both conservational and emotional — in direct proportion to its decrease in acreage. This in turn creates pressure groups, and leads me directly into the next arena.

Marketing.

Note the similarities between the rise of Marketing in business and its counterpart in birdwatching and conservation. Halting (or at least restricting) habitat destruction requires money, and this has given rise to a fund-raising culture within the conservation movement which is both vital for its future and frequently stultifying for its members. This offers a possible answer to the question — often asked — why so many bird-watchers do not belong to formal groupings; they dislike the pressure of constant fund-raising.

There is no better example of such marketing than the concept and formation of local members' groups by the RSPB that started around 1970 and is still continuing. Bringing the Society to its members by the means of dispersing its centralized mystique and of providing a frame-work around which to focus local interest, the RSPB at one fell swoop greatly increased membership income and created a structure for contin-ued fund raising. (It also sharpened an awareness of birds and bird-watching which is now in danger of subverting its original marketing intention.)

Whatever your response to such covert marketing activities, it is impossible to deny the vast increase in RSPB land holdings over my review period, a prime requirement of its Royal Charter to protect "birds and their place in nature".

Early in the period of Members' Groups culture, the RSPB contributed to a notable conservation victory when the proposals for an airport at Foulness were scrapped. This led members to think that their efforts could achieve results and gave impetus to the spread of environmental and conservational pressure groups.

This period also spans the establishment of colour television, maybe the most powerful passive marketing tool that the environmental lobby could have ever desired. Anglia Television through its Survival pro-grammes and the BBC Natural History Unit at Bristol have had an immense influence on our thinking, and such luminaries as Aubrey Buxton and David Attenborough deserve our warmest gratitude. But did we realize how this all fitted into the marketing strategy?

Of course, it may be that the strategy is itself part of the social revolu-tion. Recalling Newton's dictum that *"every action has its equal and opposite reaction"*, and speaking in psychological rather than in practical terms, I conclude that the market for wildlife films and membership of conservation bodies is merely our late 20th century response to increased exploitation, greed and destruction. Thus we must have these television programmes, take them for granted, as we do the plethora of birding books and magazines, and — to cast a glance at my original hypothesis — use them to inspire our birdwatching travels. If I appear to castigate certain overt aspects of wildlife and conservation marketing, this only reflects the level and frequency with which some conservation bodies irritate their loyal supporters with their constant expectation of financial support at the expense of birdwatching and ornithological study; but I have no quarrel with the wildlife/money equation which is, after all, the basis of the whole eco-tourism concept.

Technology.

The vast strides made in technology over this period are no better seen than in the optical equipment available to the bird-watchers of the 1990s. I currently use a pair of binoculars that (in the words of the manufacturers) combine the ultimate optical and mechanical performance with unique ergonomic design. Moreover, they are shock dampened and fully waterproof as well as being nitrogen filled for use in extreme conditions, while the unconventionally large phase-corrected roof prisms and multi layer coating ensures a bright, true colour image. (I still retain my first ever pair of binoculars, through which by comparison I can see virtually nothing.) Moreover, the modern day birdwatcher also has to use a telescope, which makes sea and estuary watching easier and the resulting records more accurate.

There is, of course, a cost implication in this quality explosion of optical technology, and latest developments seem to indicate that the higher quality of the more expensive equipment is filtering down to the cheaper models. If better quality optics lead — as they must — to better quality bird watching and bird recording, then this example of cyclical influencing is an entirely beneficial result of marketing hype.

Optical equipment aside, other aspects of technology impinge on birdwatching. The computer age affects us too, and not only in the form of computerized record keeping. Battery operated lap-tops with fax facilities open up communication possibilities undreamed of a generation ago; whilst radio pagers and cell phones linked to bird information phone lines transform sophisticated information services into ordinary and indispensible tools of the trade.

Twitching.

If I have argued that Social, Marketing and Technological factors have improved our birdwatching skills and made our records more accurate and more quickly transmitted, then the rise of twitching has fundamentally altered the focus of our entire birdwatching activities.

Twitching in its simplest form consists of watching rare and vagrant birds, wherever they occur in the country and at no matter what cost in money, time or fatigue. It is fair, I think, to say that twitching originated with a body of responsible and knowledgeable birdwatchers who looked on it merely as the icing on an already rich cake; and it is still seen that way by very many birdwatchers who practice and advocate a responsible attitude.

Twitching stems from an interest in rarities and vagrants which, in the way of freaks and rogue statistics, are of interest for the comparison they afford with the norm. Rarities and vagrants are most likely to be turned up by dedicated birdwatchers who regularly watch a particular place, or who have a highly developed sense of what a particular place will be like at a particular season. They will thus know, sometimes instinctively, when situations are different from what they are expecting, and it is this heightened awareness that often results in the discovery of rarities or vagrants. To this can be added another instinctive and understandable response — the sharing of the excitement with friends and colleagues.

Twitching, as it is understood today, goes further than this; and the excitement of the original discovery is shared via telephone birdlines and radio pagers with those others who had no hand in the discovery. Thus twitchers are watching birds that other people have found for them. Human nature, being often perverse, can trawl up primitive instincts at unexpected times. This is one of those times, and when the hunter-gatherer instinct teams up with twitching the original concept is subverted into an alternative to birdwatching rather than a value-added benefit.

Newcomers who are attracted by the founders' enthusiasm can come to equate twitching with birdwatching itself, and run the risk of creating a whole generation who never truely learnt the basics of of bird finding and ornithology. Not only does this augur ill for the future of the science, but by virtue of the marketing hype currently surrounding twitching it can also give a widespread if spurious impression that twitching is somehow superior to other forms of birdwatching. In fact, there is now a general journalistic trend of describing all birdwatchers as twitchers, and this must be vigorously discouraged

But, by contrast, it can be argued, correctly and positively, that twitching has many merits. Twitchers (or at least the original finders) have to

14

possess excellent identification skills and wide knowledge of birds from other countries. They have greatly increased the knowledge and records of vagrant and accidental birds. They have mapped significant aspects of species range expansion, for what starts as a twitch may well develop into a trend. And through a favourite pastime, bird races, they have found an ideal vehicle for fund raising and sponsorship to support conservation initiatives.

Which way to choose?

Perhaps the most important service rendered by the rise of twitching is the opportunity it affords to birdwatchers of deciding how they wish to pursue their hobby. It forces us all to review and prioritize our motives; and is no better illustrated than when a vagrant is seen by accident on a birdwatching trip where the location was chosen by very different criteria. In this serendipitous manner have Dusky warbler, Bluethroat and Zitting cisticola all given me pleasure in unexpected locations; in marked contrast to the one great practical drawback of twitching, that by the time you get there the bird may have gone.

I have always preferred the technique — in existence for far longer than twitching — that is grounded in a knowledge of how bird activity and movement are likely to vary according to season and habitat, the technique of the original bird finders. Over the years outdoor activities afford a unique sense of the wheeling of the seasons, and an obvious opportunity for comparison. This is of particular significance to anyone who belongs to a bird club and who, especially, has the task of planning the club's programme of field meetings. Such arrangements cannot be based on the instant world of twitching, and must rely on longer-term seasonal variations and comparisons.

My own involvement in programme planning, and its resulting influence on my approach to birdwatching, came about as a direct result of one of those Marketing factors which I elaborated above. 1970 was designated European Conservation Year. Not only did this bring Conservation as an issue to the attention of a wider audience, it also formed a focus — co-incidentally or not — for the RSPB's policy of Member Group formation.

Broxbourne is a town in Hertfordshire some 30 miles to the north of London, and the centre for the Members' Group in whose formation in 1971 I was involved. Lying in the valley of the River Lea, Broxbourne was — and still is — an excellent centre for local birdwatching. In the valley are water meadows and gravel pits, whilst on the hills to the west are the ancient mixed woodlands of Wormley and Northaw, and the open heaths which in the early 1970s were only just being planted with conifers. Thus the local birdwatchers could count on an impressive local list — Smew and Goosander, Little ringed plover and Kingfisher, Woodcock and Nightjar, Redstart, Wood warbler and Nightingale. The interest was there already and the Group virtually formed itself.

Even before the completion of the motorway network, Broxbourne was a good base from which to plan a programme of field meetings, and from which to acquire a feel for the cosmic movement of birds, season by season. Hertfordshire is comparatively close to the coast of East Anglia, a coast ideally located to receive waders migrating to and from their Arctic breeding grounds, and if the weather is right, or — more accurately — wrong, to attract and trap falls of vagrants and common birds alike.

The nature reserves on the north coast of Norfolk could always provide sufficient interest to keep my members happy; and Snettisham and Titchwell, Holme and Holkham, Wells and Cley became — and still are — amongst my favourite sites. But it didn't take us long to realize that these locations are by no means best in the breeding season. Though of course many interesting and significant birds do breed here, these wonderful places come into their own during winter and migration. Two examples will give a flavour of these places and explain my love for them.

No birdwatcher would consider the Knot to be a rare species, let alone the object of a twitch. Yet stand on Snettisham's shingle at the edge of the Wash in a raw February nor'easter; watch the swirling clouds of Knot as the ebbing tide moves them off their inland high tide roosts to their feeding grounds on the vast mud flats now being once again uncovered. As you marvel at this wildlfe spectacular unfolding before your very eyes, remember that the Wash, that large bite out of England's east coast, is a staging post and wintering ground of incalculable importance for a significant proportion of the world population of this species.

If winter is the time for Snettisham, September is the time for Titchwell Marsh. The RSPB have transformed this coastal marsh with adjacent beach and sand dunes into a model of its kind, attractive to such breeding rarities as Bittern, Marsh harrier, Bearded reedling and Little tern. Yet its sequence of lagoons, with controlled water levels and a salinity that increases towards the sea, is immensely attractive to passage waders, especially on their more leisurely southward journeys of Autumn. In mid-September it is frequently possible to see as many as 22 species on the reserve — from the delightful first-Autumn-plumage juvenile Curlew sandpipers on the freshest lagoon, to Sanderling, Turnstone and Black-tailed godwit at the edge of the sea. If a rarity should chance to turn up amongst them, so be it, and the twitchers will probably see it. But I, and many like me, will have gone to Titchwell that day to witness a spectacular gathering of passage waders. That can be guaranteed; the rarity can't.

Moving onwards.

I am by no means the only birdwatcher to have learnt his trade in an RSPB Members' Group; nor am I alone in leaving the Group system as skills develop, sensibilities deepen and study preferences alter their focus. I moved on in response to a profound change in my approach to birdwatching. Whereas part of my motivation in joining the Group in the first place was certainly social, my increasing attention to the scientific aspects of birdwatching and conservation led me to choose a more solitary approach, and to replace a coachload with as many chosen companions as would fit into a car.

Moreover, my attention was already being directed towards the phenomenon of variety, of the diversity that would soon absorb me totally. Great oaks from little acorns... and my first little acorn was planted when I went in search of those birds that were not to be found conveniently close to Broxbourne, and when I began to wonder by what processes of adaptation Dippers and Puffins involve the dedicated Home Counties birdwatcher in such long journeys.

Thus began a love affair with Wales. I love the hanging sessile oak woods haunted by Wood warblers, Pied flycatchers and Redstarts. I love streams like the one which flows through the valley at Bodnant Garden, and which is patrolled by breeding Dippers who vie for attention with the riotous display of azaleas and rhododendrons for which the Garden is better known. And I love the great sea cliffs of Anglesey with their platoons of nesting Guillemots and Razorbills, with Puffins strutting on the grassy tops, and — if you know where to look — with the most southerly breeding colony of Black guillemots, Tysties (in the Shetland vernacular) paddling away in the clear sea with their scarlet feet.

Minsmere.

My list of criteria for choosing birdwatching locations continued to grow. Selecting by habitat and by season, selecting by birds in a different geographical location ... so far so good; but when I came to consider the effect of habitat variety on bird variety, my best location was right back in East Anglia.

Minsmere, on the greensand Heritage coast of Suffolk between Southwold and Aldeburgh, is a tribute as much to ornithological diversity as to the enlightened conservation policies under which the reserve was established. I cherish the retrospective irony of my absorbing the basic principles of such diversity without at the time fully realizing their implications. For when, much later, I came to consider the priciples of diversity in Costa Rica, diversity based on habitat, altitude and climatic criteria, I found all the basics in place on a learning curve that had its beginnings at Minsmere.

For example, six species of tit can be seen at Minsmere within its woodland variety. Mention adaptive radiation and the average bird-watcher stares at you blankly, not knowing in sound-bite form of the process whereby closely related species evolve to exploit a variety of eco-logical niches. Yet the tits on the British list give as good and as simple an example of adaptive radiation as you are ever likely to find. After that the special adaptative requirements of, say, Great spotted woodpecker and Bearded reedling are simplicity itself. And the significance of the RSPB's conservation policy resolves itself into one whereby the Society maximises the variety of conditions and opportunities for adaptation.

Their management scheme includes the protection of an extensive if fragile reedbed, and the maintenance of habitats that range from sea and coastal dunes, through shallow brackish lagoons to mature mixed wood-land and acid heath. In so wide a range of habitats the conditions for adaptation are varied indeed, and the range of birds staggering. Little terns nest on the shingle. Avocets jostle for room on the lagoon (the famous "Scrape") with the ubiquitous Gadwall and the occasional Spoonbill day-tripping from Holland. The reedbed is famous as much for protecting the severely dwindling Bittern as for the rehabilitation of the Marsh harrier, while Bearded reedlings (number one on the wants lists of all visiting American birdwatchers) ping and whirr their way amongst the reed stems. Through the scrub and woodland, warblers delight and frustrate with their varied songs, Redstarts and all three woodpecker species occur, and even Hawfinches occasionally turn up. Visit the reserve towards the end of May, after the Spotted flycatchers and Nightjars have arrived, and you have the chance of arguably the best day's birdwatching in the whole United Kingdom.

Serendipity and the Dusky warbler

Which brings me, by a very circuitous route, back to the Dusky war-bler of this chapter's title. I hope I have by now established that the prin-ciple factor motivating my birdwatching is the pursuit of diversity; diver-sity by location and by season, diversity by geography, and diversity by habitat. (I also hope, though it is not a major objective of this book, to have demonstrated why I choose not to pursue the activities of a twitch-er.) There remains one more episode to recount, one that neatly brings all my themes together, and demonstrates the additional diversity that can flow from unusual weather conditions.

The meterological map for 1800 hrs on 16th September 1984 shown at the end of the chapter showed a high of 1024 millibars lying over Scandinavia and a cold front approaching across the British Isles from the west. These classic conditions for a fall of migrants produced a north east wind to bring in the birds and drizzly rain and mist to confuse them on arrival.

On the assumption that such conditions in mid-September on the north Norfolk coast could well be interesting, but not searching for any particular bird, I set out a first light to work the understorey scrub in Wells Woods, where the bushes were alive with warblers, tired and disorientated by the dismal weather.

My attention was attracted to one bird and in particular to its long supercilium, for the supercilium can often be the clincher when identifying unusual autumn warblers on England's east coast. This particular supercilium was long and uniformly buffish, well defined both behind the eye and in front where it appeared to taper to a point. These factors, combined with such others as its neutral grey-white underparts, its thin bill and neat head shape, its buff undertail coverts and the rounded tip to its tail, revealed this bird to be a Dusky warbler, a long-distance vagrant from Siberia, rare but not unheard of in the UK.

Remember this happened in 1984, before twitching had fully assumed its current craze proportions and before the pager and the phone birdline had taken over from the local cafe as the source of all information. On this occasion the phone at the cafe had apparently been kept busy since the arrival and original discovery of the Dusky warbler; for it was only when I was on my way back to the car, secretly gleeing at the thought of so wonderful and unexpected a find, that I ran into the twitchers who urgently asked me if it was still there. I hope they saw it; for compare the lot of a twitcher who went to Wells with the express intention of seeing a Dusky warbler and failed, with my equal and quite opposite experience.

I had not set out with the intention of seeing a Dusky warbler, and on this hangs my whole contention. The expedition was based solely on my knowledge of good bird locations by season and by habitat, and on the expectation that bad weather conditions can often be very good. So much is objective fact. But seeing the Dusky warbler added the extra element of joy, joy such as I referred to in my Prologue, joy at the unexpected, and joy that transformed my day by proving that birdwatching can truly touch the emotions.

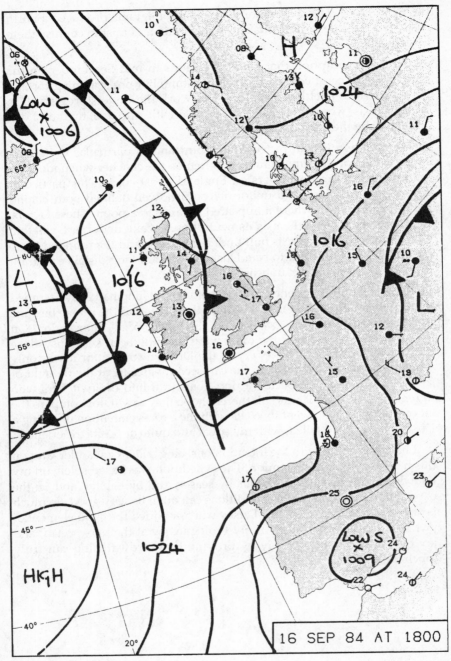

16 SEP 84 AT 1800

Crown copyright

CHAPTER 3

THE DEAD SWALLOW AND THE HOOPOE LARK

If I had not chosen to travel in search of birds, I should have had to choose to travel for its own sake. To some people, myself included, the theory and mechanics of travel are endlessly fascinating. I have always enjoyed poring over timetables and maps, especially those minutely detailed sheets published in France by the Institut Géographique National that not only show physical shading to complement the contours, but also give the population against the smallest of towns. I cannot be alone in experiencing a sensation approaching anticlimax when a minutely planned and eagerly anticipated trip appears to go by too quickly for what ought to be full and proper enjoyment; a phenomenon with which I have come to terms by the simple expedient of deriving almost as much pleasure from the planning and the reminiscing as from the trip itself.

My interest in travel per se is a natural progression from my interest in geography, an interest that goes back to that childhood birthday when my grandfather, Frank Oldaker, gave me an atlas. This quickly became a treasured possession, a Pandora's box full of wonderful names — Lofoten, Borneo, Brahmaputra, Popacatepetl. To an 8-year-old these seemed just as seductive as the shapes of the land masses — the big fish (North Island, New Zealand), the boot and football (Italy and Sicily) and the dog with the lolling tongue (Alaska). But my favourite was physical geography, and contour lines held a particular fascination for me, especially when I learnt at school how to convert a contour pattern into a side elevation view. Mountain ranges, marine trenches, and volcanoes — all kids like disasters! — these are what kept my nose in a book when others were out playing football. (As an aside of genetic relevance, I rejoice to think that as I write these words my own son is studying for 'A' level geography; the lineage is still running true.)

Travel for its own sake is to me a curiously ambivalent experience, not least for the fact that standing in, say, North Island, New Zealand bears no resemblance to standing on the big fish, whatever the Maori legend may say. The act of standing in one of my seductive shapes sees a childhood ambition fulfilled, yet at the same time my inability to appreciate the shape of the country leaves me with an irrational unease that no amount of travel experience can completely erase. So I put it to the back of my mind by bringing the true purpose of my travel to the front, and find I am incapable of travelling anywhere without studying the bird life. Travel with a purpose, when that purpose has to do with a passionate and absorbing interest, is the cure for my unease; and the Minsmere legacy — the study of bird variety in relation to habitat variety — fine-tuned the focus of my study.

Luck was on my side when my sister took up residence in the USA shortly before I discovered my interest in ornithology. Now she feeds three species of Nuthatch in her Alabama pine wood back yard. Three

21

species of Nuthatch, when we have but one in the UK that immediately begs a question. Two species — the Red—breasted and the White-breasted — are common and widespread throughout North America, whilst one, the Brown-headed, is severely restricted to pine woods in the southeast USA. The questions are beginning to pile up. Some years later in the pine woods of highland Arizona I came across three species of Nuthatch again; the two common species as before, but this time the rare and restricted species was the Pygmy nuthatch; and though a question did come to mind, the question itself began to create the glimmer of its own answer, an answer touching on conditions for species separation and subsequent evolution in isolation.

Though undoubtedly true, it is specious to say out of context that travel broadens the mind; yet the nuthatch question does serve to show how my thinking on avian diversity began to develop. Parallel to the questions came many other experiences that began to build up my collected thoughts. Having the UK as my baseline for habitat conservation and bird protection, I found it of immense interest to see how the same basic problems and human responses fared in different countries. Two countries in particular will serve as examples where I treasure — if that is the right word — two powerful and contrasting images, one negative and the other, thankfully, positive.

The live wheatear and the dead swallow

It's early April and I'm in Malta, a real fish-shaped island. I'm birdwatching on that part of the north eastern peninsular — the fish's tail — known as L-Ahrax. It's hot, much hotter than home would have been on the same date. Bees buzz in the low ground cover of vetches and clovers in the scrubby rocky cliff-top vegetation. Salicornia bushes and small pine trees vie with each other to reach my chin; and all this against a background of riotous yellow from the bushes which my Maltese friend, Ray Galea, calls acacia and which I call mimosa. I expect we're both right.

It's a perfect day, made even more perfect for this Englishman by my escape from the less predictable perfection of early April in England. It's my first visit to the Mediterranean, and I am rejoicing in my first Hoopoe and Black-eared wheatear. This latter species, of the black-throated eastern race, presents me with no less than three elegant males in gorgeous breeding plumage, the apricot on the crown and back contrasting with the white forehead and the black on ears, throat, wings and tail. Fortunately the white rumps flash a message of familiarity to remind me of my earlier awakening to their Northern relation on similar rocky scrub in the Outer Hebrides.

These pleasant experiences — both the new and the remembered — are harshly interrupted by the next bird I see. Lying on a rock in the full

22

glare of the sun is a swallow — dead, with its left wing blasted off, and I feel a sudden chill as if a cloud had veiled the sun. I am desolated by the sight of this little corpse, and as John Donne's bell tolls for this one swallow, I feel it tolling for me — and am diminished by it.

This episode is outrageous testimony to the marksmanship of a local bird-shooter; for Malta is a country where those who study and protect birds are outnumbered 10 to 1 by those who shoot and trap them. This is a country where entrenched and irrational traditions prevail, in total contrast to our northern attitudes. This is a country that resents what they see as the imposition of outside and alien attitudes towards bird protection. This is a country where visiting birdwatchers are in danger of becoming targets themselves; where live ammunition is available alongside fishing line and bait in local shops; where bird ringers can occupy one side of a valley and bird shooters the other, both in a nature reserve; where bird shooting hides face south — to greet the incoming spring migrants as they cross the Mediterranean out of Africa. This is a country, in short, that runs the risk of creating a bird-free environment.

Small wonder is it then that birdwatchers tend to shun Malta despite its huge potential as a migration watchpoint; and small wonder that the future for Malta's birdlife looks bleak, despite unassailable local optimism. Yet it need not be so.

Lark signs waymark the desert

My abiding interest in physical geography has fuelled my interest in plate tectonics, and the effect that this has had on the present face of the earth has led me to southern Israel, where one such effect is clearly visible. Tectonic movement created the Rift Valley in East Africa, as well as the Red Sea that is tearing Arabia away from Africa. The Rift continues up the Gulf of Aqaba to the southern Israeli resort of Eilat. Here it crosses onto land again, and continues northwards, via the deepest below-sea-level depression on the earth's surface — the Dead Sea — eventually to lose itself in the mountains north of the Sea of Galilee, the most northerly Rift Valley lake.

Immediately north of Eilat lies that part of the Rift known as the Arava Valley, a predominantly flat, arid desert floor separating at a distance of some ten miles two mountain walls of lunar desolation. This is a desert of stones and rocks, dotted with drought-tolerant vegetation that includes accacia bushes at their northern limit. In a featureless landscape the kilometer marker posts along the main road are the only reference points.

Yet to the surprise of every visitor the desert is not devoid of life. This surprise is its chief fascination, and larks are its main component. One of the great thrills of desert birdwatching is to witness the early morning display of the Hoopoe lark. This large, pale attenuated lark is well adapted to its desert existence. At rest, its sandy buff plumage provides excellent camouflage, but it is in display that its other characteristics serve it well. As it launches itself into the air from a perch, so you see its black and white wings and hear its plaintive but far-carrying flute-like whistles. In such a flat and featureless landscape, sight and sound carry far, and here the Hoopoe lark is in its supreme element. Since before the time of the Essenes the desert has encouraged mysticism and, some would say, hallucination; nevertheless, there is a powerful if fanciful temptation to look on this bird — in Laurence Durrell's powerful phrase — as the embodied spirit of the place.

But how does the birdwatcher find his way around this flat and featureless desert? The answer is a very practical one and provides the "good news" in contradistinction to the dead Maltese swallow. On a regular basis, the International Birdwatching Centre in Eilat (IBCE) hosts ornithological meetings. In order to prevent their visitors from losing their way in the desert, the IBCE have waymarked the trails for them, the markers being small lark silhouettes on low posts. Follow the larks and not only do you not get lost, but you also visit the best bird areas.

In juxtaposing the dead swallow in Malta with the lark-silhouette waymark signs in Israel to make my case, I find it hard to imagine two more contrasting attitudes towards the visiting birdwatcher, or a greater gulf in the understanding of eco-tourism.

At this point I came to realize that the old chiche is true and that travel was broadening my mind in ways I had never previously imagined. Not only were my travels interesting in their own right, they were opening up to me questions of scientific, moral, social and economic complexity — questions in fact that demand a chapter of their own.

CHAPTER 4

FARMING THE FOREST FOR THE FUTURE

Eco-tourism as a concept is poorly understood, especially by those who merely equate it with East African safaris and the urge to point camcorders at lions and elephants. There is, of course, much more to it than that.

Like it or not, there are many who see eco-tourism as the way forward in our enjoyment of the world's wildlife riches. Our better understanding of these riches, an attainable objective of eco-tourism, will — we hope — lead to their protection for future generations. Simply and starkly, what is the point of our studying the world's biodiversity if we are not equally concerned to see in place a framework for its future security?

As we saw in the last chapter, the examples of the dead swallow and the Hoopoe lark encompass questions of international bird protection and eco-tourism. I believe that these questions are inseparable if we are to face the future with any degree of confidence.

The background

The global view, from a late 20th century standpoint, divides the world in two — North and South, "Haves" and "Have nots", "developed World" and "Third World" — a dichotomy that was at the very heart of the 1992 Rio conference on global conservation.

"North" tends to be the temperate, richer, more developed countries typified by the G7 industrial grouping. "South" tends to be the tropical and poorer, less developed countries that over the centuries have been — and continue to be — victims of varying forms of Northern imperialism.

Given the greater diversity of tropical than temperate species, it follows that more species exist in the South than in the North, and that a greater potential exists in the South than in the North for these species to be endangered. In very general terms, the South contains resources — riches, if you will — that the North with its greater industrial, financial and political muscle has always been willing and able to extract. This is a situation that justifies itself on the principle of exploiting resources that have always been looked on as as unlimited.

Thus, to cite one example, is Malaysian rainforest exploited to satisfy the Japanese demand for plywood shuttering and disposable wooden chopsticks. Thus, to cite another, is Amazonian rainforest exploited for mineral riches and for cattle pasture to satisfy the North's craving for hamburger.

Northern financial imperialism being what it is, the producer countries — and the individual producers in particular — receive generally inadequate payment for this exploitation, despite the efforts of Traidcraft and the belated guilt complex of a few northern conglomerates. Inadequate

25

payment in turn gives rise to further habitat destruction as local people plant more cash crops in a frenzied but quite understandable attempt to boost their own economies.

It doesn't take a very profound knowledge of ecology to infer the catastrophic effect that this exploitation and destruction have on wildlife. Moreover, there is much to suggest that the human attitudes that lie behind this exploitation flow more from the Biblical assumption that Mankind — as of birthright — is to dominate Nature, than from a Darwinian assumption that Mankind — being, after all, merely a part of Nature — is equally susceptible to exploitation and destruction. (For proof, look no further than the people who live on sandbank islands in the Bay of Bengal and who drown in floods induced by Himalayan deforestation.)

Nature, despite its almost infinite ability to regenerate is, after all, finite; and species, once rendered extinct, cannot regenerate. In this way, exploitation is slowly but surely killing the planet, aided — albeit tacitly — by Mankind's capacity for greed and indifference.

But — and it is a very big but — Mankind with the big brain is also capable of rational and compassionate thought. This gives us the opportunity, if we wish to take it, of considering and implementing the alternative to exploitation — sustainable development. We have a tendency, probably motivated more by guilt than any other emotion, to look on this as using resources that have been grown especially for the purpose; but artifacts made from tropical timber and marketed to uninformed consumers differ little in principle from bananas marketed in the same way. Look on sustainable development as harvesting the wheat rather than eating the seed corn, and if the principle is still elusive, consider an actual case that neatly epitomizes the whole issue.

The Cameroon Mountains are an Endemic Bird Area in the BirdLife International definition of the term. Its unique birdlife includes Bannerman's turaco, Grey-necked picathartes and the Mount Kupe bushshrike; but it is being threatened by the activities of the local community who cut timber for use and sale, and who hunt the forest animals as bushmeat. In 1987 BirdLife International (then known as ICBP) launched the Kilum Mountain Forest Project, in the Cameroon Mountains EBA. Its programme of sustainable development set out to show the local people that such a concept could encompass a viable lifestyle, and included a scheme to collect and market honey from the flowers of the forest trees. I find this arguably the most perfect example of sustainable development, not least for the fact that it works in practice on the ground in Cameroon.

In 1991, BirdLife launched the Mount Kupe Project, similar to that for Kilum Mountain. From the times of the very earliest settlers, Mount Kupe has been central to the culture of the local people who hold it in awe as

26

the source of health and wealth, bad luck and death. BirdLife saw it as crucial to the Project's success that the local people should be actively involved. They for their part had already noted reduced water levels and increasing scarcity of bushmeat species; and were persuaded to adopt a more sustainable approach. Thus the Project is promoting a tree planting scheme to replace that which is cut, is experimenting with the domestication of several small bushmeat species, and is encouraging the spread of mushroom farming to help replace a total dependence on hunting.

How much is a bird?

But honey and mushrooms are recognizable commodities, based on their excellence as foodstuffs, and as resources are certainly older than Homo sapiens. We know honey, are happy with mushrooms, and can see their economic benefits both to producer and consumer. The conceptual problems arise when we look to treat wildlife itself as a similarly sustainable economic resource.

"How much is a bird?" is not an easy question to answer. In the terms of its Royal Charter, the RSPB is required to protect "birds and their place in nature." It follows that if birds can, in a manner of speaking, be "farmed" by the protection and management of their habitats, they can begin to be seen as a sustainable economic resource. From this point it is but a small step to use birds as flag-ship species in the basic eco-tourist argument. Birds are more widely studied and therefore better understood than any other form of wildlife. They have aesthetic as well as scientific appeal, and they are spread more widely over the surface of the earth than most other interesting life forms. They therefore make images — both the actual and the metaphorical — that fit easily into environmental marketing campaigns. What is more, the general principles of ecology should ensure that a habitat maintained and protected for its bird life will also protect the other life forms that it contains. Protect the one and you protect the other, though this view is not as cast iron as it once was. I find it logical, then, in considering the principle and practice of eco-tourism, to use birds as my principal examples. And, of course, people.

Eco-tourism at work

In the Mount Kupe region of Cameroon, eco-tourism is another way of increasing income for the local community, one that does so in a sustainable way simply by relying directly on the good state of the forest and its wildlife. Destroyed habitat and impoverished fauna are the preserves of the campaigning environmental journalist, not the prime locations for the cash-paying eco-tourist. Thus BirdLife International are actively encouraging eco-tourism, and bird tour companies are beginning to include the area in their programmes.

Eco-tourism is a contract working at many levels. At its simplest and bluntest the tourist pays money in exchange for a wildlife experience; but at a deeper and more subliminal level the tourist pays money in order that the wildlife experience shall be there at all — and shall continue into the future. Those who purchase such experiences go shopping in the same way as they might buy shoes or asparagus; that is, they select the best deal based on their own criteria. Now the dead swallow and the lark waymark signs begin to appear in their proper context. Who, given the choice, would choose to watch birds in a land where all birds are shot at, when the alternative is a land where birdwatchers are welcomed and assisted in their search?

The criteria on the eco-tourists' shopping list are many and varied, and it is likely that value for money will rank high in a sphere as subjective and emotional as a personal response to birdwatching. The spirits of Walter Rothschild and Frank Oldaker still walk with us, though the intervening years have changed our collecting habits into those more connected with life lists than with museum drawers. But whilst the collecting instinct is still as strong as ever, collecting for its own sake soon becomes stultifying unless we do something with the data that we collect. Walter and Frank used their collections to delineate subspecies and clines. We, their inheritors, use our lists both implicitly and explicitly to help us come to terms with global ornithological diversity. It is then but a small step to the BIG question "Why are birds distributed the way they are?", but that is a matter for Part II.

Into Costa Rica's cloud forest

To keep us firmly and positively in eco-tourist territory, ask another question, say, "How can I get to see a Resplendent quetzal?" This charismatic bird is a trogon occurring as two races each in its own highland region of Central America, one from southern Mexico to northern Nicaragua, the other in Costa Rica and Panama. Not only does this say much about distribution and subspeciation, but it also points to such practical matters as airlines, hotels, visas and security. Costa Rica is a country well prepared and happy to welcome visiting birdwatchers who go to the Monteverde cloud forest for a glimpse of this sumptuous bird. Though Costa Rica is by no means the only country with good eco-tourist credentials, it does it very well and being small is able to concentrate effort. Costa Rica will therefore serve very well as an exemplar for the industry.

The mission statement that they appear to share with all other good eco-tourist countries is this. *If we protect our wildlife and make it easy and pleasant for overseas visitors to view and enjoy, the foreign exchange revenue they generate will enhance the national economy which in turn will enable us to protect more wildlife.*

We are now getting to look at the other side of the eco-tourist contract — what will eco-tourists get in exchange for money, and why should they go to one country rather than another? The holes in the net of generalization are too large to confine such minutiae, so let us abandon generalization and examine one specific case.

Consider the basic choice facing Giovanna Holbrook, the visionary instigator, owner and driving force behind Selva Verde Lodge in the Caribbean Lowlands of Costa Rica. Having bought 500 acres of primary rainforest should she clear it and put it down to cattle or fruit? Or should she develop its inherent qualities and characteristics into a focus for recreation and for the study and enjoyment of the natural wonders that it contains? That she chose the second option is evidence not only of her concern for the environment, but also of her sound economic common sense; for if eco-tourism is to work it must be founded not on romanticised idealism but on on sound financial principles.

Having done her sums, Giovanna realized that she could get a better return on her investment — albeit in the loger term — by running Selva Verde Lodge as an eco-tourist destination than by farming cattle or bananas on the land. By following her chosen course she is maintaining the environmental integrity of this vastly important habitat, and is encouraging the local people to see the wildlife as a sustainable resource. There is in fact a network of cause and effect similar to that which binds all parts of the ecological equation, and thus a web of life applies just as much to the methods of supporting wildlife as to the wildlife itself.

The study of wildlife in an eco-tourist context demands that the experiences must have a focus. This can be as general as *The rainforest experience* or *Aspects of rainforest ecology*, or it can be as specific as *A study of adaptive radiation in Caribbean slope tanagers* or *The effects of topography on the speciation of wrens and aracaris in Costa Rica*. It doesn't matter what the focus is provided there is one.

Take away the focus and the trip becomes just another holiday, where greed and selfishness run the risk of destroying the very resource that attracted the visitors in the first place. There is always the danger that this perception will predominate, if for no other reason than that there are more potential customers for the hedonistic "tropical paradise package" than there are for true eco-tourist experiences. But skillful handling at local level can lure even hedonists onto river boat excursions where the sight of toucan, howler monkey or iguana can divert their thoughts along unexpected highways.

■ An interesting aspect of Eilat

We can take comfort from some research emanating from this southern Israeli resort. It has two distinct sides. On the one hand it is promoted as a prime location for winter sun, conveniently close to the large European market. This, of course, affords many opportunities for promoting snorkelling on a superb coral reef in addition to all the other major resort attractions. On the other hand its very location at a key point on an important flyway makes it the best migration watchpoint in the Western Palearctic and a magnet for birdwatchers.

However, a closer look reveals that on the whole birdwatching doesn't contribute much to Eilat's economy. But as an "add-on" benefit that creates a "green" image it may well be an important if unconscious factor in attracting visitors, even if many of them do not actively participate in the ornithological activities. Behind this may well lie the implication that general tourists prefer a resort with the environmentally friendly image associated with high profile birdwatching, the corollary being that in time they will come to expect it as the norm. This is of immense significance, for it could pave the way to reducing the environmental greed and selfishness with which so many resorts are currently viewed. It augurs well for the future of eco-tourism per se, and lays the foundation for increasing its constituency.

CHAPTER 5

TWO SIDES OF ONE COIN

In the last chapter I dealt with two of the issues (international bird protection and eco-tourism) that flow from increased ornithological awareness, which in its turn is brought about by increased travel. It is now time for me to turn my attention to the paramount ornithological travel experience — the discovery of endemism and diversity. Viewed in logical sequence, this will lead into Part II of this book where I describe the causal forces behind these phenomena.

In this chapter, however, as I continue the account of my increasing personal awareness of ornithology, I prefer to limit my description to how I came — almost by accident — to discover endemism and diversity for myself. All significant learning processes are sequential, one fact leading to another; and it is sensible to suggest that discovering the existence of endemism and diversity in the first place will quickly arouse interest in their causes. In my own case, the logical sequence is even more pronounced, for it was my interest in bird protection and eco-tourism that led me directly to the discovery of endemism and diversity.

"Neo-Darwinism" is a convenient shorthand expression used to explain how contemporary evolutionary biologists view Darwin's insights in the light of post-Darwinian thinking. Stephen Jay Gould, Professor of geology and curator of fossil invertebrates at Harvard University, is the most influential modern popularizer and commentator on evolutionary biology. He has speculated on the part played by contingency, that is pure chance, in biological evolution, and in like manner I can say with certainty that it played some part in the evolution of my own thinking and understanding. In the early years of my travels I never consciously sat down to plan the course of my ornithological development. At first the ideas of overseas locations suggested themselves to me more in terms of fantasy and pipe dream, but after a while the propositions became more achievable if still in no more logical sequence.

In due course opportunity and circumstances combined, in a good example of Gouldian contingency, to see me off to Hamilton, New Zealand as a delegate to the World Conference of the International Council for Bird Preservation (now known as BirdLife International), where bird protection and eco-tourism would feature on the agenda. In case this should turn out to be my only trip to New Zealand, I determined to spend at least some of my time birdwatching; and in doing my homework I stumbled upon the two crucial facts.

The first is simply that the birds of New Zealand are very different from anything I was accustomed to in Europe, North America or the Middle East — the diversity concept. The second is that many of New Zealand's birds, like the familiar Kiwi and the far less familiar Stitchbird, occur nowhere else in the world — endemism was upon me. These are

31

well-known facts, yet here was a situation where learning by discovery is more lasting and important than teaching by rote.

When I therefore came to combine these two concepts with what I had already seen with my own eyes and read in books, the principles of bird distribution around the world began to fall into place, and both endemism and diversity appeared to me as the two sides of one coin.

First, the Obverse — Endemism

An endemic species is described by BirdLife International as one with a restricted range, 50,000 square kilometers being the general upper limit. I am cautious in my use of the word "general", since species that are endemic to islands are as likely to be restricted by the finite dimensions of the coastline as by the biological and ecological constraints of ranges on larger land masses.

New Zealand, in common with every other relevant location, is a good place to follow the practical organizational dictum *"If we go for the endemics we'll pick up the others along the way."* Thus I planned my trip by placing a list of key endemic species against the normal travel constraints of time and distance. Kiwi, Stitchbird and Kokako headed the list, but as Kokako is the subject of Chapter 9, I now propose taking the Kiwi and Stitchbird experiences as examples of endemism at work in a real world.

Kiwis in Waitangi Forest

The Kiwi is New Zealand's most unique bird, and also its most ancient. It is a member of the Ratite family which, along with Emu, Cassowary, Ostrich and Rhea, occur in the southern hemisphere. This suggests its arrival in what is now New Zealand prior to the break-up of the ancient southern land mass of Gondwanaland. (See also Chapter 7, page 55)

Those unfamiliar with kiwis are surprised to learn that there are three species; the Little spotted and the Great spotted, both with very restricted ranges indeed; and the Brown kiwi whose range encompasses the whole of New Zealand with races specific to each of the main islands — North, South and Stewart. Kiwis are mainly nocturnal which makes them difficult to see. Maybe this explains why the majority of New Zealanders, who go so far as to call themselves "Kiwis", have never seen a kiwi outside the numerous reversed-day-night kiwi houses.

A visiting birdwatcher with limited time and a wish to see kiwis in the wild is well advised to concentrate on the Brown kiwi and should refer to a remarkable book. Stuart Chambers is one of a large number of knowledgeable and helpful New Zealand ornithologists. His book — *Birds of New Zealand; a locality guide* — sets out to make it easy for visitors to find the very special birds for which his country is famous.

I read that Brown kiwis are widely available throughout the country, but those that are the easiest to see — at Mason Bay on Stewart Island — are also the most difficult to reach. The best alternative are those in Waitangi Forest in Northland inland from the beautiful Bay of Islands. I drove for four hours up Highway 1 north of Auckland, and made my base at the resort of Paihia on the Bay.

Waitangi is famous as the location where the Maoris and the British signed the Treaty in 1840 which effectively created the modern state of New Zealand. The nearby Waitangi Forest is mainly a plantation of exotic (ie introduced) Radiata pine and this presents an anomaly. Plantations of exotics, like other forms of man-made environmental rearrangement, are generally inimical to New Zealand's native birds; and their presence in any location can be taken as some measure of the quantity and quality of native bush. By contrast, the Brown kiwi thrives in the exotic surroundings of Waitangi's Radiata pines.

In his book, Stuart Chambers gives detailed instructions for a 2-day search. I followed these by making a daytime recce for places where I hoped Kiwis were most likely not only to occur but also to be seen. I located an expanse of forest floor which looked suitable, being relatively free of undergrowth tangle and close to a convenient bank to sit on. I noted its position and returned at dusk, more in hope than in expectation but buoyed up by that sense of optimism that never seems to desert bird-watchers.

At 8.55 pm just as the sun was setting (this was late November, the austral spring) I began hearing the call of the Morepork, the local race of Boobook owl, and started sporadically playing a tape-recording of Kiwi calls, both male and female. Within 10 minutes I heard the other-worldly shriek of a male which, in the darkness, caused more than a frisson when I realized that the tape machine was turned off! The flashlight beam directed at the shriek revealed the bird not 10 yards away, shaggy furry feathers, long bill, black button eyes and all.

Kiwis evolved during the long period when there were no ground predators in New Zealand. In consequence they have little fear as they go about their business, noisily turning over the leaf litter and undergrowth tangle with their enormous feet in their search for earthworms. These they locate by smell, to the accompaniment of much diagnostic snuffling, through nostrils uniquely situated at the distal end of their long bills. Even when they are not calling they are noisy and easy to locate; but for some two hours after sunset they are particularly vocal, to the astonish-

33

ment of anyone listening in. In Chapter 11 (Page 98) I discuss the shriek of the male; suffice it now to contrast it with the very different strangled gargle of the female, which I heard less frequently.

The Brown kiwi is a good example of a New Zealand endemic bird which despite its strange evolution and habits appears to be well adapted to its particular life-style, even to the extent of thriving in exotic surroundings. This, you might say, is an example of an endemic bird surviving despite the effects of human activity. The tale of the Stitchbird is very different, showing an endemic species surviving because of human activities, and demonstrating the part played by proactive conservation in maintaining an assemblage of unique species.

Saving the Stitchbird

The honeyeaters form one of the dominant and most characteristic families of Australasia. In New Zealand this family is represented by the endemic Tui, Bellbird and Stitchbird. The Tui and, to a lesser extent, the Bellbird have been able to adapt to the human pressures on their environment, and are still quite common on the main islands. By contrast, the Stitchbird has a more exclusively nectar dependent diet, and is thus more vulnerable to changes in habitat. As a result of this, as well as of feather collection for Maori cloaks and of the introduction by Europeans of rats and other predators, by the end of the 19th Century the Stitchbird on the main islands was facing extinction.

It is at this point that the basic geography of the New Zealand archipelago assumes importance, and the concept of "Lifeboat Islands" emerges. New Zealand numbers many hundred of islands within its total land area. Some, like Macquarie and the Kermadecs, lie far off in the surrounding ocean; while others lie just off shore. All have the convenience of intervening water and discrete coast lines, both of which are important for conserving endangered endemics. Islands assume "Lifeboat" status when they are used by proactive conservation bodies to receive translocated endemic species that are endangered on the mainland.

It goes without saying that Lifeboat islands must be free from the dangers that threaten on the mainland; but it also follows that the smaller offshore islands, whether by size, topography or difficulty of access, have been unsuited to major habitat destruction for agriculture or other human activities. Nevertheless, some human contact has brought threats from introduced predators, and a major prerequisite has been the eradication of these threats. The New Zealand Department of Scientific and Industrial Research have been much preoccupied with the eradication of rats; but the best known and best documented case is the eradication of feral domestic cats from the 7,544 acre Little Barrier Island, 30 kilometers off shore in the Hauraki Gulf, north east of Auckland. To Little Barrier Island was the Stitchbird translocated, and though some tentative populations occur on other predator-free islands, this remains its world stronghold, documented as such in all world checklists.

The Stitchbird exerts a powerful attraction for birdwatchers, local and visiting alike. Viewed objectively, the bird is a valid and unique species and the subject of a concerted conservation effort. Viewed subjectively, it touches the emotions with its rarity value and its defiance of extinction. All serious visiting birdwatchers are therefore consumed with determination to see it, in inverse proportion to the almost insuperable difficulty of getting to Little Barrier Island at all.

The first difficulty is the understandable reluctance of the Department of Conservation to issue visiting permits to any but bona fide naturalists; but here a little by gentle pressure from BirdLife International friends, with whom I was planning to visit the island, helped enormously. The second difficulty is one of logistics — there is no regular or scheduled service by boat, plane or helicopter that links the island with the mainland, and no alternative to chartering a vessel from the small port of Sandspit, no easy task from a desk in England. But as with most other difficulties, when they are overcome the results justify the effort. The choppy two-hour crossing was made all the more memorable by the presence all around of Little blue penguins, Cook's petrels (which only nest on Little Barrier Island), and no less than three species of shearwater — Buller's, Fluttering and Flesh-footed.

It was not until we arrived at the island that we realized that our difficulties were still not over. In calm seas visitors transfer from ferry to launch which, in the absence of jetty or landing stage, is winched up a slipway. We arrived in conditions which were, naturally, too rough for the launch. Transferring from ferry to inflatable rubber coracle — try that some time amid the differential rocking of two craft in 4-foot waves — we paddled in ever-decreasing circles to arrive drenched on the beach; but all the optical equipment survived!

Nothing could remove the elation and sense of achievement as we arrived safely, albeit wetly, at such an ultimate destination. Theoretical study of endemism is all very well, but there is no substitute for practical field experience — permits, charters, wet clothes notwithstanding. Nor is there a better way of understanding the restricted range concept of endemism than arriving on a small island to study its endemic birds.

The rest was easy. As the result of the proactive conservation measures, Little Barrier Island is a paradise of pristine native bush, free of predators and man-made rearrangements, attractive alike to its existing and translocated endemic birds. Kakas (the North Island forest parrot)

35

flew over to greet and, no doubt, vet us, and the trees were alive with singing Tuis, Bellbirds and Grey warblers; but though delightful they were not the object of our quest.

Stitchbird we found with almost embarrassing ease and as close as the trees at the edge of the bunkhouse clearing. At 20 cms the Stitchbird is much the same size as Redwing or Northern Oriole with which European and American birdwatchers are more familiar. The male has striking plumage. The velvet black head has white tufts behind the eyes, whilst a band of yellow crosses the breast below the black of the head. The brown wings have a conspicuous white bar at the base of the primaries, and the remaining feathered parts are tonings of olive-brown. As with other hon-eyeaters the bill is decurved, and its diet of nectar places it in the select group of avian pollinators.

It is an attractive and distinctive bird, and one that is well worth the effort of saving from extinction. The actions of New Zealand conserva-tionists, who act to save their endangered endemics, add considerable weight to a BirdLife International contention. From a detailed analysis of bird distribution, they have concluded that adequate protection of the most critical areas for biodiversity will ensure the survival of a dispropor-tionately wide variety of birds. In the story of the Stitchbirds on Little Barrier Island we see this theory in microcosm.

Orangequits in Jamaica, a new slant on endemism

I have already mentioned the part played by contingency in the evolu-tion both of life and of my own ornithological understanding. Contingency or, if you prefer, co-incidence played a striking and immedi-ate part in the development of my understanding of endemism. At one and the same time it showed me the close relationship between endemism and diversity, and — in my continuing metaphor — flipped the coin to display its reverse side.

A delightful and enthusiastic member of the group with whom I visit-ed Little Barrier Island was Ann Sutton from Jamaica, the wife of Robert Sutton to whose ornithological expertise I pay tribute in Chapter 11. It was as a result of my friendship with Ann that in due course I visited Jamaica and began to view endemism in a way that would not have been possible had I restricted my travels to New Zealand.

Jamaica is a small island of 4,244 square miles (10,991 square kilome-ters), making it slightly smaller than the state of Connecticut and roughly half the size of Wales. In so small an island it is amazing to find no less than 27 endemic birds, a statistic confirmed by the 6th edition of the American Ornithologists' Union checklist. This concentrated phenome-non inspired David Lack to write his seminal work "Island Biology, illus-trated by the land birds of Jamaica", and features in Part II of this book.

Looking at endemism from the viewpoint of diversity, it is interesting to note that six of these 27 species are endemic at the generic level; but of those six, four — the Jamaican owl, the Yellow-shouldered grassquit and the two Streamertail hummingbirds — represent taxa that are familiar elsewhere. Of the two remaining, even the highly endangered Jamaican blackbird is classified within the New World Orioles (Ictiridae).

The last species — the Orangequit — is a real oddity, defying all attempts at accurate classification, and earning the following entry in the Dictionary of Birds: *A small Jamaican passerine bird of uncertain affinities, tentatively placed in the sub-family Thraupinae (see TANAGER).*

Uncertain of affinity it may be, but the Orangequit is an interesting and attractive bird, and one that involved me in an unusual discovery. Much the same size as a Goldfinch, its more streamlined form shows that it really is nearer in classification to tanager than to finch. In the bright Jamaican sun the male's blue-black plumage appears a much brighter blue, and the rectangular russet-orange patch on its throat convinces some that this is how it gets its name. The bill, slightly decurved, is black as are the legs and lores. It is considered locally common; and frequents gardens, open woodlands, roadside bushes and the borders of clearings in the wet mid-level and mountain areas, but is rare in the hot lowland areas. It feeds on nectar and fruit from low to medium trees and shrubs and comes readily to feeding stations.

I had no real clue as to the origin of the name until one day, my thoughts far distant from Orangequits, I chanced on a flock of some 60 Yellow-billed parrots (also endemic to Jamaica) busily feeding in an orange tree. This colourful and exotic sight was made all the more interesting by the fact that the birds were tearing open the fruit to get at — not the flesh as I had assumed — but at the pips which they were devouring voraciously. Robert Sutton was with me at the time; he commented that in a lifetime of watching birds in Jamaica he had never observed such behaviour before. Nature's economy takes care of the wastage of orange flesh in a tidy way. Attending the parrots, but less conspicuous in their more subdued plumage, was a small party of Orangequits who were busily consuming the flesh that the parrots were leaving. Hence their name.

Flip the coin, the reverse — diversity

David Lack showed that a study of Jamaica's land birds could answer some of the questions relating to endemism; yet a further study of island biology reveals a trend of comparatively empoverished fauna compared with continental neighbours. This is as true of the British Isles as it is of Jamaica. According to the AOU checklist the Jamaica avifauna only comprises 256 species of which 101 (39%) are resident and 27 (10.5%) endemic.

To appreciate how important Jamaica is in understanding the relation-ship between endemism and diversity, consider the fact that 21 of the 27 endemics are only endemic at the specific level. The obvious corollary is that these birds have congeners elsewhere. Two Jamaican endemics are Tyrant-flycatchers of the Myiarchus genus — the Sad flycatcher and the Rufous-tailed flycatcher — a genus containing 22 species that range north to the southern USA and south to Bolivia. A further look at the Jamaica checklist reveals nine other Tyrant flycatcher species of varying status and affinities.

Birdwatchers from the Old World are generally unfamiliar with Tyrant flycatchers, since this is one of those interesting assemblages of birds that evolved in the western hemisphere and at which I shall be look-ing more closely in Part II.

The 375 species in 90 genera are widely spread over the Americas from the tree limit in northern Canada southward to Patagonia. They probably originated in tropical lowlands, and in the Neotropical realm they are numerically the dominant land-bird family. They range in size from the smallest passerine species (Short-tailed Pygmy-tyrant; total length 5 cms, wing length 3.0 to 3.5 cms) up to such comparative giants as the 23 cm Great kiskadee and the 21 cm Tropical kingbird. Their overall colouration is drab, often olive-green above, bright or pale yellow to whitish below, with a variety of eye-rings, stripes and wingbars. Some like the aptly-named Ochre-bellied flycatcher are less ornate than the average; others like the fan-crested Royal Flycatcher or the exquisite Scissor-tailed fly-catcher are more so. Major names for members of the family include tyrant, tyrannulet, kingbird, phoebe, pewee, flatbill and elaenia.

This one family can quite easily come to epitomize the concept of diversity; diversity of habit and of habitat, of size, plumage variation, geo-graphical range and comparative frequency. And yet 2 species within the assemblage are endemic to a small island in the Caribbean half the size of Wales.

Building a nest in Costa Rica

My visits to Jamaica brought me to a watershed in the development of my ornithological thinking. I remembered my roots in England where my early preference for birdwatching by season and locality allowed me to understand and benefit from a greater diversity than is afforded by twitching. I remembered Malta and the bird-shooting culture that awak-ened me to the urgent need for international bird protection; and I remembered the early lessons in eco-tourism that I learnt in Israel. And with amazement I recalled the powers of contingency that took me in the first place to New Zealand and via New Zealand to Jamaica; and which in both countries powerfully introduced me to the phenomenon of endemism.

As I sat on my watershed contemplating the strange twists and turns of the path that lay behind me, I made a decision that the unstructured nature of my development to date had to stop, that I should adopt a more focussed approach to these phenomena that I had discovered by chance. I needed more practical experience of diversity.

Great Britain, the off-shore island, is actually a poor place to study diversity; and, despite a greater variety of woodpeckers, so is most of western Europe. North America, where I had travelled extensively, is better but enormous and difficult to handle in practical terms. I determined that now was the time to take the plunge and tackle the Neotropics, the faunal region with the greatest diversity on earth. But again, as always, those practical considerations of travel — time and distance — rose up to confront me, and pointed me in the direction of Costa Rica.

No one should tackle Costa Rica unprepared. Consider its basic appeal. Here is a country two thirds the size of Scotland, and roughly the size of West Virginia, containing more bird species than the whole of North America. In Part II I examine some of the reasons for this amazing situation. Suffice it here for me to state the geographical basics. Two coastlines, Pacific and Caribbean, separated by a mountain spine, in a narrow isthmus that allows interchange of land species between the two adjoining continents. Though simply stated the effects are colossal and at first difficult to comprehend. A detailed appraisal appears in Part II, but let me make a start based on explaining the general by considering the particular. Tyrant flycatchers again. In Jamaica there are nine species from five genera. In Costa Rica there are 78 species from 41 genera. The implications of this bald statement are fabulous indeed, but this is a chapter for experiences rather than explanations.

Moving still further away from the general to the particular, one of the flycatchers in Costa Rica gave me more pleasure than all the others. The Common tody-flycatcher is well named. Occurring from southern Mexico to eastern Bolivia, it is abundant in Costa Rica where two races are recognized. It is a small bird, and at 9.5 cms slots in size between the larger North American kinglets and the smaller European "crests". In the adults the forehead, forecrown, lores and upper cheeks are black which shades to dark sooty-grey on the nape and to dark olive-green on the rest of the upperparts. The wings are blackish with pale yellow edges, the tail feathers black tipped with white and the whole of the underparts entirely yellow. This is a small dainty bird, in the field appearing black and yellow, which in the way of all small birds is constantly busy and on the move. Our paths crossed many times throughout Costa Rica; but many of the sightings were transitory, and the one that was not printed itself on my memory.

Tiskita is so remote, in the far south west near the frontier with Panama, that it can only be reached by a single-engined plane. The grass airstrip, the one flat area, links the palmfringed Pacific beach to the encroaching rain forest up the hill. In a small grove of trees that led to the beach a pair of Common tody-flycatchers were building a nest. From my English birdwatching I am familiar with the bottle nest of the Long-tailed tit, and from Sweden with the nest that gives the Penduline tit its name. Weaver-birds and Oropendolas are other birds that construct intricate hanging nests; but I had never before watched such a nest being produced.

The completed nest of the Common tody-flycatcher is described as an elongated, hanging structure with visorshaded side entrance and loose tail dangling below a rounded chamber, of most varied vegetable materials, bound with spiders webs and well lined with feathers, seed down etc; 3 to, rarely, 100 feet up at the end of a slender twig or hanging vine.

I never saw the completed nest; but I sat and watched, entranced, as the two little birds constructed both the sling attachment and the upper ring from which the chamber would eventually hang. I was no more than 20 feet from the foot of the tree, yet the birds continued undisturbed, oblivious of all else but the need to build a nest, the need — over-riding all others — to pass their genes on to the next generation.

While I watched them I fell to musing. However far we travel, however varied our experiences, however many birds we see, the present moment is merely the minute interface between the future and the past. The birds we are watching right now represent the same interface between all the birds we have ever watched in the past and all the birds we hope to watch in the future. It is only possible to experience that which is passing in front of us in this minute time window, and that is why the present moment acts as a burning glass to focus all our attention onto the birds at the end of the binoculars. The Tody-flycatchers were as totally absorbed in their activity as I was in mine, and thus we shared a moment of union as strong as if they were sitting on my hand. Small wonder that the experience is so deeply etched in my memory.

In Jamaica, the Sad flycatcher is common in the gardens around the Great House and in the pastures beyond; its familiarity allowed me to use it as a yardstick against which to compare the other species; and its song — if such it can be called — was the first I ever recorded. In Costa Rica, amid the riotous Neotropical diversity, it took one pair of Common todyflycatchers to focus my mind and attention onto the eternal truths that lie behind the science and the theories and the personal experiences.

Such adventures of the mind and soul are the stuff of real experience. They give a better understanding of the theoretical and intellectual intricacies of endemism and diversity, and ease my passage into Part II.

PART II

DIVERSITY AND ENDEMISM EXPLORED

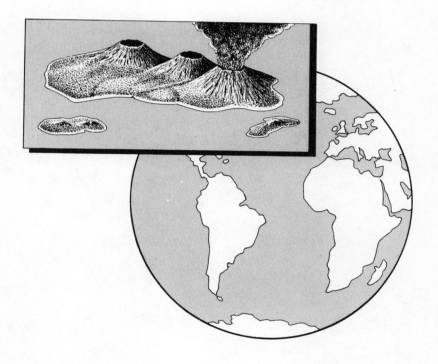

CHAPTER 6

GODS OF CREATION

Things that go bang in the night

Geologists and tourists alike find it a thrilling experience to spend time in close proximity to a volcano. There are almost as many reasons for finding volcanoes exciting as there are people to experience them, reasons that vary from the profound to the superficial, and from the scientific to the emotional. American and Filipino geologists were responsible for monitoring the development of Mount Pinatubo's eruption and for advising the local populace on the right time to evacuate the area so as to maximise safety and minimise panic. There is no doubt that they would add terror to the list.

Some people rationalize their excitement at volcanoes as merely an extension of their love of mountains, others claim that the response is overtly sexual. Some (mostly geologists) choose a theoretical study of the elemental forces that continue to shape the world we live in, others risk life and limb by taking measurements and samples from the craters. Others still simply marvel from the gut at phenomena that are easier to observe than to comprehend.

Anyone contemplating a visit to Costa Rica will find that volcano visits feature high on the itinerary. The country contains over one hundred volcanoes, most of them inactive; but some, like Poas and Arenal are demonstrably active. Poas is 2704 m high and in May 1989 shot ash a mile into the air, though currently (1993) quiescent to the extent of merely producing acid-like rain and sulphurous gases.

Vulcanologists recognize three main types of volcanic eruption, and the 1989 episode represents the Plinian type. These are not ordinary eruptions in the sense of discrete bangs, being sustained jets which may continue for minutes or hours. Strombolian eruptions need not concern us here; but the third type, Vulcanian eruptions, are wholly relevant to my story.

Vulcanian explosions are discrete bursts that take place at intervals of minutes to hours, and need to be personally experienced to allow their full enormity to sink in. Arenal is one such volcano. 1633 m high, conical and voluptuous in her volcano-ness, she rises abruptly from the tropical vegetation of Costa Rica's northern Caribbean slope. (Psychologists might like to comment on why volcanoes are generally referred to as female.) Her arrival was nothing if not dramatic. Until the beginning of July 1968, Arenal was a low hill covered with dense vegetation. Heralded by slight earth tremors, the forest began to steam and smoke, and women washing clothes in the nearby streams noted with some surprise that their water was hot!

On 29th July all hell — literally — broke loose and Arenal exploded, hurling red hot boulders and molten lava onto a largely unprepared countryside. Vulcanologists have calculated that rocks were propelled up to 5 kms from the vent and created impact craters many metres across. Standard ballistic theory suggests that supersonic ejection velocities of approximately 600 metres per second were necessary to achieve this, while the atmospheric drag in still air was countered by the shock wave generated by the explosion. The official death toll was put at 62, which in local opinion was understated, and 5 square kilometers of agricultural land were totally devastated.

To understand the true vulcanian character of Arenal it is necessary to visit her now. She has been erupting continuously since 1968 and is generally considered to be one of the most active volcanoes on earth. This is of great interest to the Smithsonian Institution who have established an observatory close by, 1.5 miles away across a reassuringly deep valley. The measuring equipment is connected to a television monitor where shock waves are graphically transmuted into oscilloscope traces amid an excitement that never seems to dim with familiarity.

A tourist lodge has been incorporated into the Observatory, and now visitors can experience this ultimate volcano experience in relative safety. It is not unusual for there to be immense eruptive bangs at 2 hourly intervals throughout the night — vulcanian to the nth degree — and many tourists find their sleep patterns interrupted. A more restful activity is to sit in wonder on the terrace; to watch lava flowing down the sides, suddenly glowing extra red as the nose breaks off, to admire plumes of magenta fire thrown thousands of metres into the sky, and to share a moment of communion with the ancients who may after all have got it right by worshipping volcanoes as the gods of creation.

It is no co-incidence that these elemental forces of creation are available for all to see in Costa Rica, a country that is teeming with natural diversity; nor it is by accident that I have chosen the example of Volcan Arenal to introduce that part of my story that seeks to explain some of the causal forces that lie behind this diversity.

Diversity on a Plate

To understand how volcanoes work, and how their formation contributes to the worldwide diversity of birds, my chosen exemplars of general biodiversity, we now have to start looking more closely at this world of ours, this Planet Earth, and to consider it for a moment in terms of geology and geophysics.

The Earth, as we know, is a ball with a central core superimposed by successive layers until the surface is reached. The central core is divided into an inner and an outer section along the line where changes occur in the physical properties of iron, a major constituent of the earth.

Temperature and pressure combine to control the strength of a solid; heat diminishes its strength and compression increases it. The pressure at the earth's inner core is so great that despite the high temperature iron is in the solid state; whereas beyond the dividing line the temperature and pressure are sufficiently balanced to allow iron to liquify.

Moving outwards, and occupying depths between 2,883 and 350 kms, there exists an area known as the mesosphere ("middle sphere") where temperature and pressure are in equilibrium and allow iron to exhibit both great strength and great temperature. Above the mesosphere (350 to 100 kms deep) the balance between temperature and pressure changes once again, giving the rocks little strength. This plastic zone is known as the asthenosphere ("weak sphere").

The top 100 kms are known as the lithosphere ("rock sphere") and incorporate the uppermost part of the earth's mantle and all of its crust. Here the character of the rocks changes again, making them cooler, stronger and more rigid. This is of particular significance since these rocks can only with difficulty be broken or deformed, compared to the ease with which this can happen in the underlying asthenosophere.

The critical point to remember about the lithosphere is that it is not a continuous sheet, but is broken into a number of very large plates.

The theory of **Plate Tectonics** was proposed as recently as the 1960s, and in the short time since has sparked a revolution in modern geological thought. The theory considers that as a result of the earth's internal convection the lithospheric plates are in constant motion, at speeds of up to 10 cms a year. The plates slide sideways, in some places colliding to form mountain ranges, in others splitting apart to form new ocean basins. The Himalayas are a good example of the former, the Red Sea of the latter.

We have a tendency, arising from the extreme slowness of geologic time and from the immensity of the issues involved, to view the earth as an entity, static and immutable. Yet everything on the earth's surface, submerged and exposed alike, arises as a direct or indirect result of the lithospheric plates drifting raft-like on the surface of the more plastic asthenosphere. The complicated motions involved, some visible, some not, are given the term tectonics, a word derived from the Greek *tekton*, a builder or carpenter.

A source of confusion arises from the term **Continental Drift**, often but erroneously used as a synonym for **Plate Tectonics**. Though closely related there is an essential and quite literally underlying difference between the two terms. If Continental Drift can be defined as the theory that the continents once formed a solid land mass and have very slowly drifted to their present positions, Plate Tectonics provide a physical explanation of how this can have taken place. This distinction is important in understanding what follows.

Marginal action

Since there is more than one plate in the lithosphere, it follows that the plates must have margins. Geologists recognize 3 types of margin — two are of passing interest to my story, the third is central to its importance. Let us consider the two less important margins first:

— Divergent margins (spreading centres) are fractures in the lithosphere where two plates move apart and allow new crustal material to emerge. A good example of this is the plate margin that runs down the the centre of the Atlantic Ocean and which continues to this day to pull it apart.

— Strike-slip margins (transform fault margins) occur where two plates slide past each other. This is the most frequent location of earthquakes.

The geological unfolding of my story requires a close attention to the third type of margin. As the name implies, *convergent margins* occur where two plates move towards each other. In this situation two things can occur:-

— the two plates collide in what is, naturally enough, referred to as a collision zone. Thus are many mountain ranges formed, such as the Alps and the Appalachians, and a current developing collision zone occurs west from Papua New Guinea to Timor in Indonesia;

— one plate sinks beneath the other in what is referred to as a subduction zone.

Students of geology can read of subduction zones in a very clear exposition by Brian J Skinner and Stephen C Potter in their book *The Dynamic Earth*. I cannot improve on their words:

"Near a spreading centre, the lithosphere is thin and its boundary with the asthenosphere comes close to the surface. This thinning of the upper mantle and crust happens because magma rising towards the spreading centre heats the upper mantle and crust, and only a thin layer near the top retains the hard, rigid strength properties of the lithosphere.

As the lithosphere moves further from the spreading centre, it cools and becomes denser. Also, the boundary between the lithosphere and the asthenosphere becomes deeper, and as a result the lithosphere becomes thicker and the asthenosphere thinner. Finally, about 1000 km from the spreading centre, the lithosphere reaches a constant thickness and is so cool that that it is more dense than the hot weak asthenosphere below it and starts to sink downwards. Like a conveyor belt, old lithosphere with its capping of oceanic crust sinks into the asthenosphere and eventually into the mesosphere. The process by which the lithosphere sinks into the asthenosphere is called subduction, and the margins along which plates are subducted are called subduction zones. They are marked by deep trenches in the sea floor.

As the moving strip of lithosphere sinks slowly through the asthenosphere, it passes beyond the region where geologists can study it directly. Consequently, what happens next is partly conjecture. On one point, however, we can be quite certain: The lithospheric plate does not turn under, as a conveyor belt does, and reappear at the spreading edge; rather, it is heated and slowly mixed with the material of the mantle. The thin layer of oceanic crust on top of the sinking lithosphere melts and becomes magma, and some of this magma reaches the surface to form volcanoes. As a result, *subduction zones are marked by an arc of volcanoes parallel to but about 150 kms from the trench that marks the plate margin."* (My italics)

This is an elegant dissertation on an important subject, and leads to a vital link in my chain, namely that land bridges are created from subduction zones by means of volcanoes. But before I run too far ahead of myself, I must now consider in more detail the relationship between Plate Tectonics and Continental Drift and the part that this plays in the unfolding drama of diversity.

Continental Drift and the breakup of Pangaea

It is now generally agreed that the present-day continents once formed a solid landmass to which the name **Pangaea** was given, derived from two Greek words meaning "all earth". The northern part was given the name "Laurasia", a composite word derived from Laurentia, the old name for the pre-Cambrian core of Canada, and Eurasia; while the southern part was called Gondwanaland, a name derived from a distinctive group of rocks found in central India. When seeking evidence to show that India and the present-day southern hemisphere continents originated in the same landmass, it is of interest to note that similar rocks to those found in India are also found in Africa, Antarctica, Australia and South America.

An understanding of the matters with which I am now dealing demands from the reader a sense of spatial awareness and some knowledge of geology, both descriptive and chronological. It will therefore be helpful if I include at this point maps and diagrams to demonstrate in visual form some of the details I am giving:-

Fig a — Current boundaries of main lithospheric plates and the direction of their move-ment.

Fig b — Diagram of a spreading edge and a subduction zone.

Fig c — The dispersal of Gondwanaland from 200 million years ago to the present day.

For an indication of the original configuration of Laurasia and Gondwanaland, please refer to Stephen Ling's line drawing at the start of this chapter.

It is possible to get some idea of the shape of Pangaea by fitting together pieces of continental crust along the 2,000 metre marine contour. This is the dividing line between continental and oceanic crust, and neatly serves as the conceptual link between the theory of Continental Drift and the theory of Plate Tectonics.

Under the influence of the earth's internal convection that powers the action of Plate Tectonics and the resulting Continental Drift, Pangaea began to break apart at some time in the Triassic Period, some 200 million years ago. Initially the split was between Laurasia and Gondwanaland, but by the Cretaceous Period those continents that we now call Africa and South America further broke away in the more general fragmentation of Gondwanaland. That they separated in the manner and direction and to the extent that they did can be attributed to the fact that much of the intervening ocean floor only appeared as an agent of separation in the Cenozoic era, and that didn't begin until 75 million years ago.

The creation of new land

It would be very easy to assume that the configuration of Gondwanaland as it broke up was similar to the configuration of the present-day landmasses whose origins can be attributed to the original southern super-continent. Though the 2000 m marine contour jigsaw is interesting and persuasive, it is too facile an explanation and takes no account of the constructive and destructive agents working in the process of fragmentation. Erosion is an agent that is not directly attributable to earth forces; and though it has played its part in the unfolding dramas that have led to the present day atlas shapes it is not the primary source of my current interest. For this source we must turn again to Plate Tectonics and Continental Drift as agents of change.

I have shown how the actions of Plate Tectonics ensure the constant movement of materials in the earth's crust and mantle. The forces unleashed by the earth's internal convection determine the differing forms of plate margin. The divergent margins or spreading centres create new material, particularly new ocean floor; and the space taken up by this extra material is absorbed at convergent margins, which as we have already seen take two forms — collision zones and subduction zones.

At collision zones the crustal materials take a course that is highly visible and abrupt; for, in simplified terminology, it is the impact and uplift at collision zones that cause mountain ranges to be formed. By contrast, at subduction zones, where the crust is recycled into the mantle, the changes are more subtle though the forces they unleash can be spectacular. Some of this recycled crust — magma — reaches the surface to create volcanoes and, even more significantly, volcanic arcs.

In its very simplest form a volcano can be seen as a mountain, though everyone knows the difference between Mount Fuji and Mont Blanc. What is important is that both mountains and volcanoes are land forms caused directly by Plate Tectonics. Moreover, they are land forms which by being additional to the original mass and elevation have the power to alter climate by altering topography.

Thus we begin to see how it is possible for such elemental forces of geological change to affect the circumstances in which life forms can evolve, and this may be a convenient time to enumerate them.

* The breakup of Pangaea and Gondwanaland, and the subsequent dispersal around the globe of their constituent parts, not only altered the climatic zone in which their evolutionary processes were taking place, but ensured that in many cases and for long periods these processes were taking place in isolation.

* The collision zone effect further changed an already fluid status quo. By bringing one land mass into contact with another it exchanged one long sequence of isolation — oceanic — for another — altitudinal — by creating mountain uprise.

* The subduction zone effect created arcs of volcanic islands which began to encourage the interchange of mobile species between larger land masses that were previously mutually inaccessible. These volcanic arcs are the building blocks of the land bridges that complete the exchange.

* Such large scale movements of land masses and the positions where — in the terminology of our short human time span — they have come to rest, are bound to have knock-on effects. For example, a land bridge, occurring where previously there was a clear oceanic passage, will have a mighty effect on the pre-existing ocean currents; and to put this into perspective we have only to imagine how the climate of western Europe would change if the Gulf Stream were ever to be diverted away from its Atlantic seaboard.

* The uprising of mountains, whether of volcanic origin or not, is bound to create a barrier in a place where none existed before, and interrupt existing patterns of wind direction and strength. In this way the

Atacama Desert is created as a direct result of the cold Humboldt current running up the warm west coast of South America in close proximity to the Andes. The onshore breezes that push in towards a hot land are formed of air that has been cooled by traversing the cold current. On reaching the land they are forced to rise into the high coastal mountains, where they are cooled by this ascent more than the land is capable of warming them, and little water vapour is condensed. Thus the equilibrium in the system between sea, breezes, desert and mountains is maintained by the presence of the Humboldt current.

* The effect on climate of the uprising of mountains can also be demonstrated very clearly in Costa Rica. The prevailing north-east trade winds bring in moisture off the Caribbean and ensure that the eastern (Caribbean) slope of the central cordilleras is wetter than the western (Pacific) — rain shadow — slope.

* Just as it can be demonstrated that the presence of mountains, uprisen where previously none existed, has a profound effect on the climatic conditions for evolution; so it can also be demonstrated that the altitudinal variations inherent in any mountain system will create a wide variety of climates and micro-climates. This effect can be clearly demonstrated in the Andes, the longest mountain chain in the world containing some of the highest mountains. Latitude also plays a part in determining the size and spread of climatic change; in the central Andes, around the equator, the snowline occurs at about 5,000 metres, whereas at the continent's southern tip there is permanent snow as low as a few hundred metres.

Thus there exists an almost infinitely wide range of evolutionary conditions, and from this we can infer that the landmass shapes in a modern atlas favour high levels of diversity — widely separated continents and long shorelines, significantly placed mountain ranges, wide expanses of shallow tropical water and a generous scattering of islands.

An evolutionary dynamic

Powered by the energy of geophysics, the theories of Plate Tectonics and Continental Drift presuppose constant dynamic movement. Both evolution and — in its natural form — extinction are constantly dynamic processes. Survival is the mainspring of life, and evolution is a survival response to unique and changing circumstances.

Thus all life is driven by the earth's internal convection; but viewed against the short time scale of human life the movement of its dynamic is so minutely slow that an event as instantaneous as the eruption of a volcano is immediately comprehensible and seized on as significant. As the outward and visible sign of great and numinous forces it has few equals, and no one need be surprised that primitive people worshipped volcanoes as the gods of creation.

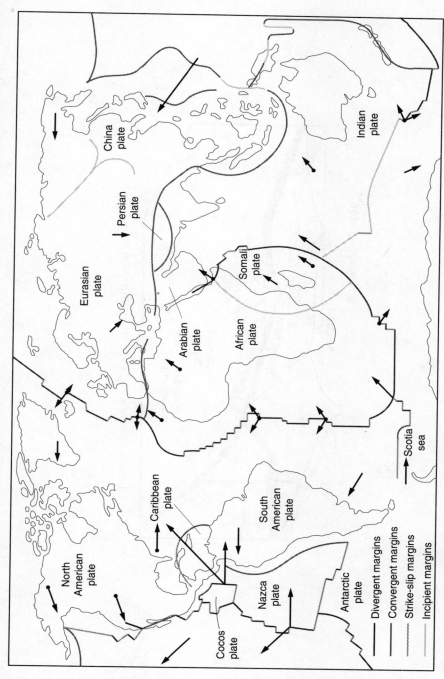

Fig a. Current boundaries of main lithospheric plates and the direction of their movement.

North
American
plate

Caribbean
plate

Cocos
plate

Nazca
plate

South
American
plate

Antarctic
plate

Eurasian
plate

China
plate

Persian
plate

Arabian
plate

African
plate

Somali
plate

Indian
plate

Scotia
sea

Divergent margins
Convergent margins
Strike-slip margins
Incipient margins

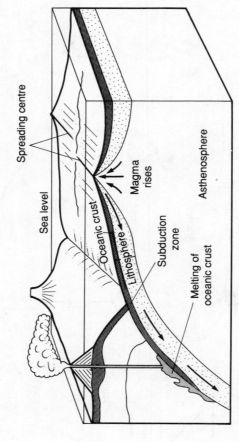

Fig. b. Diagram of spreading edge and subduction zone.

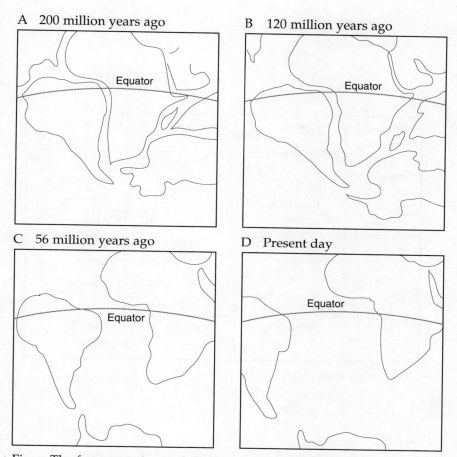

A   200 million years ago

Equator

B   120 million years ago

Equator

C   56 million years ago

Equator

D   Present day

Equator

Fig. c. The fragmentation and dispersal of Gondwanaland from
        200 million years ago to the present day.

Million years ago	Eras	Periods	Epochs
0.025	Cenozoic	Quarternary	Recent
1			Pleistocene
10		Tertiary	Pliocene
30			Miocene
40			Oligocene
60			Eocene
75			Paleocene
135	Mesozoic	Cretaceous	*Rise of birds*
165		Jurassic	
205		Triassic	

Chronology of geologic time.

CHAPTER 7

OF RAFTS AND RATITES

Darwin's log in the new light of Contingency

There is no doubt that the publication in 1859 of Charles Darwin's *On the Origin of Species* was a scientific milestone of such magnitude that it changed the course of history in ways that may only be comparable to the splitting of the atom and the discovery of DNA. The book with its beautiful if dense Victorian prose is lower down the average modern reader's list of priorities than its importance deserves; and, inevitably, the years since its publication have allowed those whom the book has influenced not only to delve deeper into evolutionary biology but to come up with amendments and alternatives in the light of their own developing knowledge.

Darwin viewed the history of life through two predominant metaphors — competition and wedges. A world full of species is analogous to wedges packed into a log; new forms can only enter by displacing others — popping out the wedges. In a situation dominated by the principles of natural selection species are displaced by competition, and those that are better adapted emerge victorious.

But competition implies a fundamental comparison, for at the very simplest level one species competes with another. Thus natural selection can only operate at the precise location where the interface occurs between these two species, and the circumstances that determine the outcome are those pertaining to that precise location. Darwin did not mean that the term "better adapted" implied any inherent anatomical superiority; merely that it reflected conditions in a changing local environment, ie the precise location of inter-specific competition.

From time to time thoughout this book I have referred to the concept of contingency. Now is the time to bring it out of the closet and subject it to the full glare of scrutiny. Evolutionary contingency is a theory popularized by Stephen Jay Gould, professor of geology and curator of fossil invertebrates at Harvard University, and can be defined as the sequence by which one event or situation is directly affected by another. Moreover, there is a crucial implication that the sequence may have arisen by chance and may not necessarily form part of a preconceived plan.

When Darwin's theory of natural selection is viewed in the light of contingency, it begins to dawn on us that the inter-specific competition that results in adaptation (or extinction, for that matter) happens as a result of random, if not unique, combinations of circumstances. Taken right back to the origins of life on earth, this concept demonstrates how unlikely it was that life should ever have originated at all, and opens the way for profound religious and philosophical meditation.

This scrutiny of contingency shows that there is a logical causal sequence linking adaptation by chance with the geological ideas of the last chapter. Excluding geophysical forces that are subject to natural laws, there is nothing in this world as quirky and unpredictable as trends in geography and climate. Continents split and drift apart, and this affects climate — both globally and locally — in two ways:-

— Firstly, a piece of drifting continental land may end up at a very different latitude and longitude from where it set out on its journey. Both its new position in relation to the equator and the angle at which the sun's rays strike it will affect its climate, and this is no more graphically illustrated than by the temperate location of Antarctica in Triassic times, 200 million years ago.

— Secondly, changes to geographical configurations by means of mountains, volcanoes and land bridges materially disturb pre-existing patterns of wind, currents and rainfall; not to mention such minutiae as rivers that change course, estuaries that dry up and deserts that form in the rain shadow of mountain ranges.

If large scale changes are so quirky and unpredictable, it follows that their contingent effect on local environmental conditions will be just as quirky and unpredictable; and in this way we begin to detect the link between geophysical forces and species diversity.

Intermission

This book has now progressed to a point where I feel it is essential to restate my motives and issue a disclaimer or two, so that what follows can be seen in the correct context.

My aim all along has been to clarify for interested but essentially amateur birdwatchers those factors that affect the distribution of birds, so that they may have some idea of why birds occur where they do and why birdwatching travel has to be so precisely targeted. Since most of the explanations are available in the scientific literature to those with the time, patience and inclination to study them, my objective is that this book should be be a personal distillation of the basic and essential facts rather than just another text book.

Two other criteria determine my position. Very few people have had the good fortune to travel to every part of the world and thus to be able to draw on a global experience of these matters. This is why my approach has to be based on my own experiences; and, making a virtue of this necessity, this is why I prefer to use examples from around the world that demonstrate the universal trends and truths.

Here is my final caveat. No one person can possibly have a total knowledge of this enormous subject. Specialization takes care of the problem, and if I examine the matters that follow more from the perspective of geologist and geographer, those with other perspectives will have to make allowances. My aims will be well served if my readers are inspired to delve deeper and develop their own particular specialized interests.

Ratites on the rafts of Continental Drift

In terms of diversity the Ostrich represents good value. It is the world's largest, heaviest, tallest and fastest-running bird and has an eye of which the diameter is the same as the length of the world's smallest bird, the Bee hummingbird. In the context of my story the Ostrich plays a significant role by being the best known member of that group of birds known as Ratites.

Flightlessness is the key element. Having no flight requirement ratites have no need of a deeply keeled sternum for the attachment of flight muscles, and the word Ratite derives from the Latin word "ratus", a raft. Their flightlessness forces us to confront the matter of their distribution. Fig. A shows this distribution in graphic form — Ostriches in Africa, Rheas in South America, Emus in Australia, Cassowaries in Australia and New Guinea, and Kiwis in New Zealand. To this can be added the extinct species — Moas in New Zealand, Aepyornis (Elephant bird) in Madagascar and Dromornis in Australia.

Each present day landmass has its discrete species or range of species. Australia, New Guinea and New Zealand are all islands, while both Africa and South America have experienced long periods of isolation; all understandable in terms of the raft metaphor of Continental Drift. Flightlessness is a key adaptation to life on islands; gigantism is another. All ratites, except the Kiwis and especially the extinct species, are larger than one would expect. (Even the Kiwis exhibit traces of a gigantic past by laying eggs that are gigantic in relation to body weight. Typical clutches contain 1-2 eggs, each weighing 18-25% of body weight depending on the species; the inference being that the process of ovulation has not kept pace with the shrinking of the other functions.)

The word isolation (the Italian for island is "isola") holds one of the keys to the answer, but the fact that all their locations are in, or originated in, the southern hemisphere postulates a Gondwanaland origin for the ratites.

In this way we can see the beginnings of a pattern emerging, based on a presumed ancestral ratite that evolved in Gondwanaland prior to its break-up. Fig. A shows its fragmentation, with the development of those present-day landmasses that each contain discrete ratite species. Continental Drift is here working to begin the process of speciation, a process of adaptation that is further enhanced by the unique environmental conditions of isolation. This is a recurring theme in the history of diversity.

The Penguins are another example of a family with a southern hemisphere distribution and the presumption that an ancestral penguin must have evolved in Gondwanaland prior to break-up. The fossil record begins about 45 million years ago and recognizes some 32 species distributed in a pattern that is broadly similar to the present day (see Fig. B).

By that late Eocene date where the fossil record starts the fragments of Gondwanaland were beginning to assume a more modern configuration, but by then the adaptive pressures on penguins had already fallen into two categories. A similar lifestyle determined the basic anatomy and the ability to "fly" under water in pursuit of a marine diet, but the environmental pressures in the differing and individual locations of penguin evolution had ensured diversification into the 18 species recognized today.

It is becoming clear, then, that there are two major factors to consider. Geology disperses the basic species, which are conditioned to adapt for survival by the unique and dynamic environmental criteria that they find on arrival, or that develop after their arrival.

The final theme that links ratites and penguins is one of primitiveness. In the days before DNA studies inclined some ornithologists to classify birds according to their genetic characteristics and relationships, the taxonomic order was based on considerations of anatomy and morphology. By these criteria, primitive birds came first in the taxonomic order, and in a checklist typical of pre-DNA scholarship, the ratite families appear in positions 1 to 5 and the penguins in 7th position. The fact that both ratites and penguins are so ancient places them in the right chronology for a Gondwanaland origin which their wholly southern hemisphere distribution would seem to confirm.

Widespread sedentary species

For many reasons, mainly sociological, the majority of those globetrotting birdwatchers who inspired this book come from the northern regions of the world where the climate is temperate and the economic conditions conducive to study and travel. For these birdwatchers the tropics exert a powerful fascination, and many have a pre-conceived mental picture of the architypal tropical bird.

Trogons are likely candidates for this categogy, and the 39 species form a distinctive and uniform family (and order) of quiet, sedate and solitary inhabitants of tropical forests. They are all brightly coloured, none more so than the Resplendent quetzal, another of the recurring themes in this book.

Much has been written about the Trogons, but what is of concern to us here is an anomaly in their distribution that caused much angst to ornithologists until the theory of Continental Drift became generally

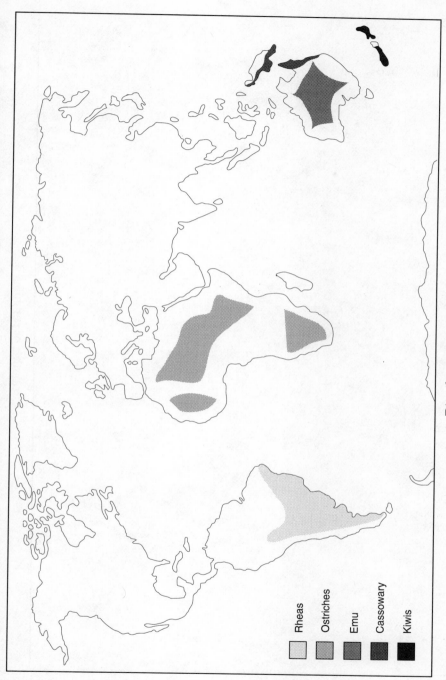

Distribution of ratites A.

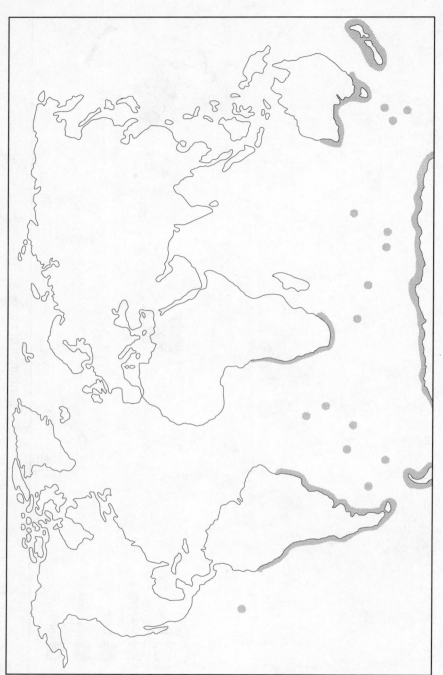

Distribution of penguins B.

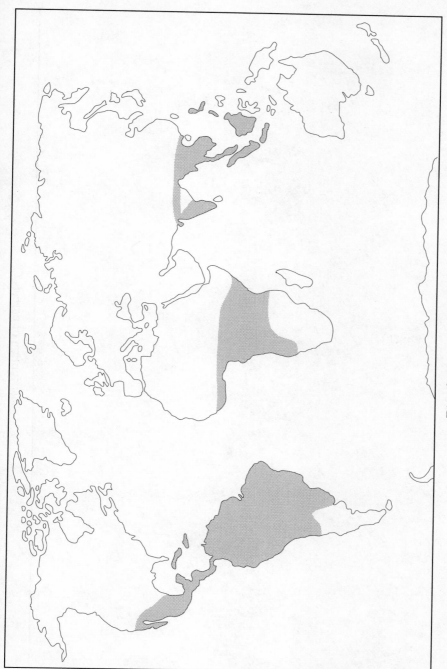

Distribution of trogons C.

Distribution of barbets C ^{2}

accepted. Though trogons are most numerous and diverse in the New World, where 25 species in 5 genera occur from southern Arizona to northern Argentina, there are 3 species in one genus in sub-Saharan Africa from Liberia to Zanzibar, and 11 species again in one genus in Asia from western India to Java and the Phillipines. This interesting and disjunct tropical distribution is curiously at odds with the sedentary and non-migratory habits of all Trogons; but an examination of their present day countries of occurrence postulates a Gondwanaland origin, with the greatest variety in the Neotropics where there was the greatest range of environmental conditions to drive adaptation (see Fig. C)

To confirm the general and to reinforce the particular aspects of this theory we must also look at the Barbets, a family that mainly inhabit tropical forests, and take their name from the feathers and bristles around the base of the bill. They are medium sized, strongly-built, thickset birds with large heads and a wide range of colours Though their basic distribution in the three faunal regions is similar to that of the Trogons, a closer examination reveals a different ground pattern. In the Neotropical realm there are 11 species in 3 genera, and in the Oriental realm 25 species in 3 genera. It is in the Afrotropical realm with 43 species in 9 genera that the greatest variety occurs, where several species have exploited much more arid habitats than those in other continents.

Hummingbirds, the swiftest fliers of all

Being English myself, I can speak for the globe-trotting birdwatchers of northern Europe when I say that the Hummingbirds are generally considered to have the most charisma of all. A significant reason for this is the transatlantic journey necessary to see them, and this immediately begs the question of their exclusively New World distribution.

For birds that start as small as the eye of an ostrich, the fossil record contains no evidence of hummingbirds for the simple reason that their tiny bodies and fragile skeletons leave inadequate imprints. Studies of comparative anatomy reveal a close relationship with Swifts, and this begs another question comparing the worldwide distribution of Swifts with the limited distribution of Hummingbirds.

Hummingbirds show such enormous diversity and cover such a huge geographical range (Alaska to Tierra del Fuego) that they must have undergone a very long period of adaptive radiation, a process that is thought to have begun in the early Tertiary period, some 60 to 70 million years ago. Present evidence suggests that the splitting of South America from Africa took place in the Cretaceous period, some 110 million years ago — that is to say, some time before the supposed origin of the Hummingbirds. The corollary is that the Hummingbirds did not begin to evolve from a swift-like ancestor until after the separation and isolation of South America.

There is also the presumption that that the swift-like ancestor existed in Gondwanaland times, and that this creature evolved into the present day Swift assemblage as the Gondwanaland fragments dispersed around the globe. The particular workings of adaptive radiation ensured that Hummingbird wings did not have to be sufficiently strong to colonize those other continents that are separated from them by oceans; whereas other and equally unique adaptive pressures endowed Swifts with powerful wings for long-distance dispersal.

Significant variations in reproductive anatomy and syringeal musculature

In attempting to unravel the causes of distribution, diversity and endemism, there is another line of thought that we should follow. It takes us momentarily away from the dominant theme of birds, but its relevance is clear.

Kangaroos are probably the world's best known marsupials, though they are but the tip of a huge iceberg of both living and extinct marsupial species. As is well known, marsupials give birth after a very short gestation period; in one species it is as short at 12 days and 18 hours, the shortest for any known mammal. The embryo produced in this way is so unformed as to be unrecognizable as a "baby" or an "infant", and instead is given the name of *neonate*. The neonate transfers to its mother's pouch (Marsupium is a Latin word meaning "little bag") where it suckles milk from a teat and grows into a properly developed young animal.

Marsupials are most generally associated with Australia, though a more detailed study will reveal their presence in modern day North America (the Virginia opossum), as well as in the fossil record of South America where they flourished until the advent of unfamiliar predators across the Panamanian land bridge. But the land bridge was not entirely their downfall, and the Virginia opossum demonstrates its distribution potential.

If we look on marsupial distribution as yet another instance Gondwanaland fragmentation, we have only part of the picture. Just as the unfamiliar predators crossed the land bridge from the north, so they were of a different anatomical structure that takes us right back to that incredibly distant time when Pangaea split north into Laurasia and south into Gondwanaland.

In Laurasia evolution proceeded in response to different contingent adaptive pressures. These gave rise in due course to the mammalian reproductive system based on the womb and the placenta that has reached its apogee in human beings. Lest we succumb to the latent hubris in that last statement, let us remember that by the process of convergent evolution (similar contingent adaptive circumstances in widely separated geographical locations) there exist — now or in the past — pairs of mammals across the anatomical divide; sugar gliders and flying squirrels, placental wolf and Thylacine, and an extinct sabre-toothed "cat" of each persuasion, amongst many others.

The split between Laurasia and Gondwanaland is also relevant to the evolution of birds, and specifically to the evolution of the Passerines or perching birds, the huge order containing roughly 60% of all living species. Ornithologists recognize two major categories of Passerines but name them according to their current response to DNA-based taxonomy. What anatomists call Oscine and Suboscine passerines, geneticists call Passeri and Tyranni (from the Latin for Sparrows and Tyrant flycatchers respectively). These divisions coincide almost exactly, and because adherents of both sides acknowledge the same distinction the differences between them occur at both the anatomical and genetic levels.

The anatomical characteristics that differentiate Oscines from Suboscines concentrate on syringial musculature — the voice box and vocalization. Thus the Suboscines, considered the more primitive, are in general restricted to less musical and more monotonous vocalizations; whilst the more advanced Oscines have an anatomical basis for their more complex songs and include such notable songsters as Nightingale, Robin and Skylark. The distinction is immediately apparent to anyone who has listened to the vocal efforts of kingbirds alongside mockingbirds. But the distinction goes further and demonstrates the true parallel with the marsupial/placental divide.

Suboscines are mainly restricted to South America, with isolated and relict outliers in the Old World (sub-Saharan Africa to south-east Asia) and Australia; a distribution that suggests a Gondwanaland origin similar to marsupials. The Oscines, now worldwide, had their origins in Laurasia, and thus run parallel to the placental mammals, even to the extent of entering South America by the same Panamanian land bridge as the unfamiliar mammalian predators. It is fanciful, if invigorating, to imagine the southward expansion of full oscine birdsong into a land where it was not previously known.

Throughout my examples there runs a thread of logic concerning the primary causes of distribution and diversity; distribution based on Continental Drift and diversity on Contingent Adaptive Pressures. Its consistency goes a long way towards answering the questions that prompted me to write this book.

A tale of vagrant Gallinules

So far in this chapter I have restricted my comments to continental landmasses, and that within the context of diversity. But the picture is incomplete without a consideration of islands and their effect on that most fascinating aspect of diversity — endemism.

Islands fall into two categories, oceanic and continental, easily understandable in the light of their geological origins. Oceanic islands take us back to the theory of Plate Tectonics and its capacity to create new land at spreading centres and subduction zones; examples being Iceland, the Azores, the Hawaiian group and the Aleutians. Continental islands are those that exist on continental shelves and have been separated from the "parent" continent by rising sea levels and erosion. Examples are Great Britain, Trinidad and Sumatra.

It is clear that the proximity or otherwise of islands to continental land masses will materially affect the life forms that they contain. In 1966 a survey of Pacific islands was launched by the Section on Conservation of Terrestrial Communities of the International Biological Programme. It was their contention that islands provide unique opportunities for studying the interaction of living things with each other and with the whole environment. All the relevant factors can be investigated and determined with exceptional precision in the simplified ecosystems afforded by islands, factors that included the origin, geology, geography, topography and climate of the site and the natural and man-made influences that have been brought to bear on it. But it was not always so. The special attraction that islands hold for us stems largely from a primitive urge to escape from the struggle for existence to a refuge where surrounding waters act both as a bulwark and a source of sustenance.

It was not until 1831 when Charles Darwin set sail in HMS Beagle that the scientific interest in and importance of islands became more clearly recognized; or until his observation of land birds on the Galapagos Islands set in train the thought process that changed the course of scientific history. By same token, the studies by Eagle Clarke on Fair Isle at the turn of the century began a process that established the importance of observatories on islands and quasi-islands (peninsulars and promontaries) in the search to unravel the mysteries of migration and distribution of land birds.

Between 1950 and 1952 studies were carried out on the islands in the Trista da Cunha group, in the south Atlantic 2,000 miles out from South America which is the continent of origin of their land birds. These islands are far distant from regular migration routes, yet during the study period nine species of vagrant land bird were recorded; while a later study on Gough Island, the most outlying island in the group, recorded six species of vagrant. Of great interest was the fact that both studies recorded the American purple gallinule, which was shown to be a regular stray in the sense that every year a few found their way to these islands.

This would seem to prove that difficulty of access and dispersal may be less of a limiting factor for island populations that was originally thought. The factors that appear crucial to the would-be immigrant are a. conditions approaching their customary ecological requirements, b. no pre-existing competitors and c. a colonizing ability. Since this last factor presupposes the presence of both males and females, this requirement is most likely to be met in flocking species; and it is no surprise that such species (parrots, pigeons, finches etc) are well represented in island faunas.

English birdwatchers, on crossing the 22 miles of the Dover Straits, remark on the greater variety of birds in continental Europe. They are merely responding to a phenomenon, long known, that island bird faunas are poorer than those of the nearest continent, even if they are at no great distance, and that this poverty is accentuated with increasing isolation. Recent studies conclude that there is some correlation between species diversity and the size and isolation of the island in question; but that the question of size is only significant to the extent that it represents diversity of habitat, a diversity further complicated by climate and topography.

Geological factors determine the location of islands, and ecological constraints are the basic factor that limits the number of species on islands. Since this is just another way of referring to my recurring phrase "contingent adaptive pressures", we may deduce that ecological constraints not only power the quality but also the quantity of species adapted to island living.

David Lack and island endemism

Jamaica has been identified by BirdLife International as a key centre for endemism, having the highest level of endemism for an island if its size anywhere in the world. Though the island lies almost equidistant from Florida, Central America and the north coast of South America and is surprisingly not very geographically isolated, its unique composition of species has perhaps the closest affinities with Central America, to which it was almost linked when sea levels were lower during the ice ages.

Jamaica is a good laboratory for studying island adaptations, and it was here that David Lack reached his conclusion that ecological limitations encourage each island species to fill a broader niche and to exclude more specialized species than would be the case with continental equivalents.

The Jamaican avifauna contains 27 endemic species, and at first sight it may seem puzzling, in view of the limiting effects of island biology, that island populations are so notorious for the number of endemics they contain. Isolation plays a part but this is not the whole story, and it will be instructive to examine the possible sequence of events that leads to endemism.

In a phenomenon known to evolutionary biologists as the "founder effect", individuals from a species (or, more probably, a population) colonizing an island are likely to possess only part of the genetic variability of the parent species, or even to possess the genetic material of the species in a ratio different to that which pertains to the species as a whole. It is this genetic difference, operating in geographical isolation and responding to the contingent adaptive pressures of a new environment, that can lead very quickly to full speciation and, maybe, to the creation of endemic species.

What happens in practice is simply that the colonists find a suitable vacant niche with novel adaptive demands. This results in a period of rapid adjustment, during which their dietary and breeding habits, along with many other aspects of their behaviour, undergo a fundamental change. It will then be only a matter of time before this manifests itself in physiological changes that lead to further changes in anatomy and morphology, and eventually in their genetic makeup. In other words, the genetic changes and the pressures of adapting to a new environment cause them to end up looking different; and we can begin to comprehend not only the difference between the Sad flycatcher, the Jamaican endemic, and the Olivaceous flycatcher, its widespread mainland congener, but also the reasons for the difference.

I can no longer delay introducing *adaptive radiation*, a concept defined as the slow evolution of body forms and behavioural patterns to suit a variety of ecological niches. Though adaptive radiation is seen to best advantage in the full diversification of mainland species, it is impossible to ignore its importance in the island situation.

Where a vacant niche is too diverse for one species to take full advantage of it, that niche is likely to be filled by adaptive radiation. In some cases, as with the honeycreepers of Hawaii, the populations expand and achieve an explosive adaptive radiation which, within the confines of islands or archapelagos, is small enough in scale to allow close scritiny and almost certain explanation.

The finches of the Galapagos, that had such a seminal effect on Charles Darwin, have radiated to the point that there is even a vampire finch which pecks at the feather bases of sea birds and drinks the blood. The radiation of these thirteen species of Darwin's finches suggests that a species invading and occupying a new island, and filling it with multiple specialized species, is initiating a process whereby later arriving species can be actually pre-empted from following a similar pattern of radiation. The small assemblage of flycatchers, mockingbirds and warblers with which the finches co-exist, have not achieved a similar depth or pattern of radiation.

New Zealand and the continuity bridge

Adaptive radiation is one response to contingent adaptive pressures; island endemism is one response to many geological factors, one of which is isolation. Thus to consider the process of adaptive radiation in the context of islands is the conceptual bridge that carries us into the next chapter.

New Zealand is the most isolated major landmass in the world, and as we have already seen it contains a bewildering array of endemic species. Those who have watched Kiwis in the wild marvel at their relationship with other ratites around the southern hemisphere. The honeyeaters, the Tui, Bellbird and Stitchbird, are related to other honeyeaters in Australia; whilst Brown teal and New Zealand falcon are recognizably related to other common families around the world. Two families — the Wrens and the Wattlebirds — demonstrate just how long New Zealand has been isolated from other parts of Gondwanaland.

The Rifleman is the best known of the New Zealand wrens. It is tiny, a mere 3 inches, and inhabits deep forests of native bush. Its primitive vocal organs produce simple nasal chirps and calls; and though it shows some similarity in structure and behaviour to pittas, its affinities are uncertain and it may be descended from some remote pitta-like ancestor that became isolated in New Zealand at the very beginning of the Gondwanaland breakup.

Wattlebirds, too, are endemic to New Zealand and it is only as a result of proactive conservation that two species survive, the Saddleback and the Kokako, the Huia having "gone extinct" in the years since 1907. As with the wrens, the affinities of the wattlebirds are uncertain, but they are believed to be offshoots of the primitive — that word again! — crow-like stock that also produced bowerbirds and birds of paradise.

Evolution in isolation has produced the birds that exist today, and the part played in that evolution by adaptive radiation neatly combines the themes of this chapter — distribution by geological forces, and diversification though contingent adaptive pressures.

CHAPTER 8

A Fabled Eldorado

Why choose the Neotropics?

To review the causes of avian diversity is a daunting task; and in both making my task easier and confining this chapter within reasonable bounds, I follow the lead of the statistician and use a sampling technique. My first decision, then, must be to go where diversity is at its greatest — the tropics — for it is here that we find in place all the principles that determine diversity and that can be applied at lower concentrations elsewhere in the world.

But why the tropics? The reasons for tropical preeminence in biodiversity have caused biologists many headaches; and in their search for answers they have looked variously at such factors as climate, solar energy, quantity of habitable terrain, variety of available habitats, incidence of environmental disturbance and the degree to which the floras and faunas are isolated. Their combined work has suggested a solution that can be relatively easily understood. This is what they term the Energy-Stability-Area Theory of Biodiversity, or ESA Theory, which can be stated as follows: the more solar energy, the greater the diversity; the more stable the climate, both from season to season and from year to year, the greater the diversity; and the larger the area, the greater the diversity.

A theoretical understanding of biological diversity, as with all other academic disciplines, is only of real value when backed up by practical experience. Thus my second decision is to choose the Neotropics for the simple reason that this is the area of the tropics with which I am most familiar.

The Neotropical avifauna exerts a powerful fascination, both on those who know it well and on those who merely perceive it as a fabled Eldorado somewhere beyond the western horizon. Consider two statistics that give a flavour of Neotropical diversity. Firstly, South America contains nearly 3,000 bird species, roughly one third of all birds on earth. Secondly, Costa Rica, a country smaller than Scotland and much the same size as West Virginia, occupies a mere 0.03% of the Earth's land surface, and contains approximately 850 species of birds or roughly 9% of all birds on earth. Both statistics take some believing, let alone understanding.

In some circumstances, and to many people, diversity is implicit in quantity; but the appeal of the Neotropics — to European birdwatchers even more than to their counterparts in North America — lies in the number of species, genera and whole families that are not found anywhere else in the world — cotingas, manakins, toucans, antbirds, motmots . . . the list seems endless.

I have another reason for selecting the Neotropics. South America is a huge continental landmass with interesting outlying islands and a crucial land bridge to the north. Landmasses imply continuity of both territory and movement, while the land bridge ensures a corridor that enhances this continuity. My consideration of these features is in marked and deliberate contrast to the "island effect" that I discussed in the last chapter.

Recapitulation

But before I begin a closer examination of the causes that lie behind the Neotropical phenomena of diversity and (by association and extension) endemism, let me briefly recapitulate my conclusions so far.

In broad but fundamental terms distribution of species can be thought of as being initiated by the geophysical and geological effects of Plate Tectonics and Continental Drift; but let me make it clear that Plate Tectonics and Continental Drift must not be inferred in sequential isolation, but are concurrent and always have been.

In the same broad and fundamental terms, diversity can be thought of as resulting from the contingent adaptive pressures on the species in the circumstances and in the places to which they were distributed. Not least amongst the changed circumstances resulting from the break-up of supercontinents were the increased length of shoreline and the shallow seas that separated newly fragmented land masses.

And finally, I take full responsibility for the phrase — contingent adaptive pressures. This combines Darwin's original concept of natural selection with a more contemporary interpretation that also views evolution in terms of contingency.

Mountains and volcanoes, yet again

For a moment we must return to Plate Tectonics, but within the confines of my study area the focus becomes more precise. A physical map of the Americas from Nicaragua southwards shows two prominent features — the Andes and the Central American land bridge. Consider their origins.

After splitting from Africa in the fragmentation of Gondwanaland, South America sailed off westwards into the widening Atlantic Ocean until its plate came into contact with the Nazca and Cocos plates which were moving eastwards. The inevitable contact caused a subduction zone that is responsible for the volcanism that characterizes the western part of both Central and South America.

The land bridge originated as an arc of volcanic islands; and the island that became the Cordillera de Talamanca, highest and most southerly of Costa Rica's mountain chains, became a major centre of endemism in its own right. The volcanoes of the Andes are not only the highest in the

66

world but have given their name — andesite — to a form of volcanic rock that is found around the world. Both the Andes and the land bridge form part of the Pacific "ring of fire", that is lit by the beacons of active volcanoes.

Moreover, the chronology of the contact is significant for the evolution of Neotropical species; and it is no coincidence that a date of 65 million years ago accords closely with the date postulated for the diversification of hummingbirds by adaptive radiation in the newly created environments.

From this subduction activity two conditions develop that are central to the understanding of distribution and diversity:-

*   Mountains arise where no mountains existed before, adding both climatic and altitudinal diversity to our equation, as well as a geographical discreetness.

*   Land is created where no land existed before, and at the land bridge a continuous passage allows interchange of land species between the vast continents on either side.

How mountains affect diversity

When mountains arise in places where no mountains existed before, the effect on evolutionary patterns is great. We should look on mountains from two spatial viewpoints, the lateral and the vertical.

— The lateral viewpoint

This explains the total dessication of the Atacama desert on the west side of the Andes, compared to the familiar image of rain forest on the wetter eastern side. This is an important principle which I shall reinforce with two further examples, both concerning the Caribbean and its prevailing north-east trade winds.

The island of Jamaica has an approximate east/west axis, which the north-east trades strike at roughly 45 degrees to the vertical. The Blue Mountains, in the eastern third of the island, rise to a height of 2,290 m at Blue Mountain Peak and receive moisture from the trade winds. Thus a rain shadow is created to the south-west of the mountains; and birds such as the Bahama mockingbird, a species that favours arid habitats, has its only Jamaican location in this area of dry limestone scrub.

In Costa Rica the mountains are higher than in Jamaica, with the continental divide peaks of the Cordillera Central nudging the 3,000 m mark. I recall leaving Ciudad Quesada on the Caribbean slope to drive the 15 or so kilometers over the divide to Zarcero. As we climbed further up the mountain road the fog got so thick that we could hardly see the tail lights of the vehicle immediately in front that was also crawling through this traffic hazard. Within seconds, literally, we drove into brilliant hot tropical sunshine, and had no need to consult the map to assure ourselves that we had crossed the Continental Divide onto the Pacific slope.

— The vertical viewpoint

Todies are interesting and appealing little birds in the order Coraciiformes, closely related to Kingfishers and Motmots. They are the only family of birds entirely restricted to the Greater Antilles, and present problems both to the taxonomist and the student of diversity. Some ornithologists contend that their differences stem simply from the island effect, others believe they represent a "super species". What is past question is their distribution; one species each for Jamaica, Cuba and Puerto Rico, and two for Hispaniola.

Since Hispaniola at 29,418 square miles is considerably smaller than Cuba at 42,804 square miles, it is not island size but altitude that determines this speciation. Cuba's highest point is 1,181 m whilst that of Hispaniola is 3,175 m; and sure enough the two Tody species on Hispaniola are separated altitudinally, one in the mountains, the other throughout much of the lowlands.

The effects of altitude on ecosystems and diversity

The Andes run the whole length of South America and claim many peaks in excess of 6,000 metres (Aconcagua is 6,959 m and Chimborazo 6,310 m). The potential for altitudinal and latitudinal variation in ecosystems is almost infinite, as are the resulting contingent adaptive pressures for avian speciation.

Above the tree line, which in the equatorial Andes varies between 3,230 m and 3,850 m, vast open spaces sweep upwards to meet the snow. From the equator north to Costa Rica these high treeless solitudes are known as paramos, tropical alpine shrubland; whilst further south in Peru the paramo gives way to the drier puna, tropical alpine grassland. Hummingbirds are generally associated in our minds with lush tropical vegetation, whilst woodpeckers cannot — we think — exist without trees. Yet in the harsh climate of the paramo and puna we find a small number of birds that are particularly adapted to the extreme conditions. Here at altitudes up to 4,600 m is the Andean hillstar, a hummingbird eking out an existence that depends on a higher than usual protein diet and a form of nightly hibernation that allows it to cope with the intense cold. Andean flickers are woodpeckers found throughout the bleak puna zone between 3,000 m and 4,900 m. They forage for beetle and moth larvae, often gregariously in flocks of up to 30, on stony slopes and level grassy areas usually in close proximity to cliffs or rocks which in the absence of trees they use for lookout posts. We may speculate on the contingent adaptive pressures that have forced these two species ever higher in the Andes to the very edge of nonsurvival, and compare them with other species round the world, for example the King and Emperor penguins, that survive and reproduce in extreme conditions.

Working our way downhill to the treeline and the highest altitude forests, we first encounter elfinwood. The trees here are stunted as much by shortage of sunlight as by low temperatures; they are short and twisted and struggle through cloud and rain to reach a height of 2 metres. The Elfin woods warbler is endemic to such conditions in Puerto Rico, and its generic affinity to the Dendroica wood warblers of North America illustrates the island effect on endemism. Dendroicas are highly migratory, and it is possible that some birds carrying less than the full genetic pontential of their species landed in Puerto Rico where they proceeded to speciate according to the sequence postulated in the last chapter.

Further downhill, we come next to cloud forest, an obviously damp habitat that encourages the growth of epiphytes, especially mosses, lichens and bromeliads. This compounds the assortment of conditions to which species must adapt. Birdwatchers visiting cloud forests very quickly learn that there is a substantial assemblage of species that is only available to them here. To many this is their first experience of speciation through adaptation, as they struggle to come to terms with the variety of redstarts, foliage-gleaners and nightingale-thrushes.

Below the cloud forests comes a forest type known as montane. This habitat is cool and moist, and proliferating orchid species join the array of epiphytes and tree ferns. Pausing in this more familiar ecosystem, it is clear that I am painting a picture of stratification; though one based on the conditions imposed by altitude and such climatic factors as rainfall, temperature and prevailing wind. In each "stratum" and, according to the precise topographical configuration, each microclimate, there exists a great diversity of individual habitats — ecological niches — that provide the species they attract with the necessary contingent adaptive pressures for diversification and endemism.

Continuing our journey downhill towards the sea, we reach so great a diversity of habitat that altitude ceases to play a dominant role, being supplanted by such factors as climate, soil type, proximity to the sea and human activity. Habitat types are as varied as savannah, dry deciduous forest, thornwood, "jungle" (disturbed or secondary growth forest), riverine food plain habitat and mangroves. All these habitats reflect unique conditions for diversification, and demonstrate the successional effect from summit to sea.

To this list we must sadly now add the habitats of human destruction for which all birdwatchers have their own names, but even here some birds flourish. These habitats arose so recently that it is not yet biologically possible to assess what effect, other than extinction, they may have on contingent adaptive pressures.

Tropical rain forest

In a temporary but important digression from mountains, I have left the most diverse ecosystem till last. Neotropical rain forest occurs in lowlands and on lower slopes. It was first described by Alexander von Humboldt (1769-1859), the German explorer and scientist who in the Classical fashion of his times named it *hylaea* meaning "forest" in Greek. His *Journey to the tropical regions of the new continent* contains the scientific observations that he made on an expedition to Central and South America. Later in the 19th Century, Alfred Russel Wallace, writing in his *Natural Selection and Tropical Nature*, described the rain forest in minute and loving detail.

In an ironic twist to the tale of convergent evolution, a concept that concerned them both, Wallace is jointly credited with Darwin as discovering the theory of natural selection; and it is now thought that Darwin brought forward the publication of *On the Origin of Species* to forestall Wallace's attempt to claim precedence with his version of the theory. Whatever the truth of this tale, it is no coincidence that Wallace should view tropical rain forest in the same context as natural selection.

A good description of tropical rain forest might be an evergreen or partly evergreen forest receiving not less than 100 mm precipitation in any one month for two out of three years, frost-free and with an annual temperature of 24 degrees Celsius or more, though seasonal variation is both typical and important in most tropical forests. Conditions for natural selection are virtually perfect.

There is no greater ecological complexity on earth than tropical rain forest, a concept which many people equate with biodiversity itself. This is no bad analogy, for if all species on earth that did not live in rain forest were suddenly to become extinct the earth would have lost a mere 10% of its total biodiversity. But though this statistic is vast in its allembracing sweep, it does after all only describe the conditions for diversity that exist in rain forest.

Everything in the forest begins with the dense and continuous mass of tree canopy. In a fundamental process comparable to the geophysical forces that have powered Plate Tectonics and Continental Drift, the canopy collects the energy of solar radiation and fixes it through photosynthesis into leaves, flowers and fruits. The forest trees soar upwards in

70

the struggle for sunlight, a condition accentuated by the new growth that rapidly fills the gap when a tree falls. The height of the trees further increases the diversity of habitats and microclimates, by providing multi-level conditions and lighting that varies from full sun to full shade. The moisture ensures a dense growth of epiphytes and creepers, and the constant temperature guarantees continuity.

The forest food chain starts with the primary consumers; with the myriads of insects that feed on juices, stems and leaves; and with fruit-eating birds (macaws, pigeons, tanagers etc) and those that live on nectar (hummingbirds). Primary consumers provide food for secondary consumers; the woodpeckers and woodcreepers that hunt the bark insects, the cuckoos that take the caterpillars, the antbirds that prey, not mainly on ants but on the creatures that the ants disturb. Over all these are the tertiary consumers, the raptors that prey on all creatures below them in the food chain — the Collared forestfalcon, the Semicollared hawk, the Ornate hawk-eagle.

Here we have a situation of security where food occurs in such abundance that every creature has a wide choice, ensuring a complex and flexible ecosystem. Let those who would destroy rain forest pause and consider what it is they are destroying, and for what short-term gain.

To me it seems logical that this digression on tropical rain forests should have intruded at that point. After all, the prime reasons for the existence of such forests are climate and altitude — or lack of it; and a proper consideration of the various ecosystems and the ways in which they affect diversity is incomplete without them.

Some other effects of topography on diversity

I now feel obliged to widen my scope to consider the more general effects of topography, not just of mountains, on speciation.

— Isolation and speciation

Speciation is, after all, the biological process by which diversity and endemism come about. Ernst Mayr defined a biological species as "an actually or potentially interbreeding population, reproductively *isolated* from other such populations." (My italics.) For this process to create speciation the flow of genes between populations must be prevented for long enough to ensure reproductive isolation, and this explains how sub-speciation is seen as a step along the same road before full speciation is complete.

(Though straying for a moment from my theatre of operations, there is no better example than New Zealand to explain how speciation is affected

71

by isolation. New Zealand is the most isolated large land mass in the world, and has been that way for at least sixty million years. It is hardly surprising, then, that New Zealand contains such a wealth of unique species.)

It thus obviously follows that geographic isolation is an important medium for fragmenting populations, and this principle is graphically demonstrated by mountains. Mountains that exist where no mountains existed before, as in the case of the Andes, present a formidable barrier within a pre-existing continuous ecosystem; and creatures on one side are physically prevented from mating with those on the other side for the simple reason that they cannot cross over. The same constraints apply to wide rivers, savannahs and deserts that are formed by geological and climatic forces; while "micro variations" in an ecosystem further contribute to the variety of sub-species and endemics.

The uplift of Costa Rica's Cordillera de Talamanca is one such isolating barrier, and pairs of closely related species exist in the rain forests of the Caribbean and southern Pacific slopes respectively — for example, Bay wren and Riverside wren, Collared aracari and Fiery-billed aracari.

— Dispersal routes

Consider a case that demonstrates how mountains relate species diversity to species distribution. The Hairy woodpecker is widespread in North America and familiar to European birdwatchers as being con-generic with the Greater and Lesser spotted woodpeckers. It is also a common resident of Costa Rican highland forests from 1,500 m up to the timberline, even though further north it is not considered a highland species. In the Costa Rican highlands it finds conditions similar to those that it favours at lower altitudes further north, and as a species has been dispersed southwards at ever increasing altitudes down the mountain chains.

The lesson of hummingbird distribution

An emotional response to the 320 species of hummingbird is to look on them as the Western Hemisphere's greatest gift to the world of birds. A more measured scientific scientific reaction is to investigate the reasons for the number of species and the extent of their distribution. The results of such an investigation add substance to my survey of ecosystems and will neatly introduce a closer look at the concept of adaptive radiation.

In South America there are 88 hummingbird genera and a breakdown of their distribution by habitat appears as Table 1.

Table 1

Habitat	No. of genera
Arid coastal zones, west/north	5
Sea level to 1,525 m (tropical level)	41
1,525 - 2,580 m (sub-tropical level)	19*
2,580 - 3,500 m (temperate level)	20**
Above 3,500 m (puna/paramo level)	3

* includes 4 genera in subtropical habitats by latitude
** includes 1 genus in a temperate habitat by latitude

The Andes demonstrate how criteria of topography, altitude, climate and especially micro-climate create the contingent adaptive pressures by which diversity and endemism can occur on a huge scale, and also emphasize the importance of these criteria to hummingbird speciation. The 62 species of hummingbird that occur at the temperate level represent the greatest number for any bird family in the Andes. This helps us to comprehend the astonishing diversity of the Neotropics, but also — by a process of extrapolation — to apply these truths to avian diversity around the world.

Adaptive radiation

Adaptive radiation is a recurring theme in this book, and it can be defined as the principle whereby birds slowly evolve different body forms and behavioural habits to suit a varying selection of ecological niches. I have looked at adaptive radiation in the context of the tit species at the Minsmere RSPB reserve as part of the process whereby I began to come to terms with diversity; and I have also used it as partial explanation of the diversity and endemism inherent in the island process. In the context of the present chapter it has enormous relevance.

I have been at pains to show that climate and topography have created an almost infinite number of micro-habitats, ecological niches, into which birds have diversified. Adaptive radiation is the biological process by which they have done so, and the ecological diversity of the Neotropics contains some of the best and clearest examples of the process.

It is easy — perhaps too easy — to imagine that adaptive radiation is seen to best advantage in the overwhelming diversity of rain forests; but the importance of this tends to be magnified and distorted by the high profile given to rain forest by the environmental protection lobby. Whilst it is impossible to deny that rain forest conditions are ideal for the proliferation of diverse life forms, true biodiversity is dependent as much on variation between habitats as on variation within habitats; and this is a principle just as relevant to Minsmere as it is to the Neotropics.

The cotingas, a diverse family of sub-oscine passerines which, from a heartland in tropical forests along the Amazon and in southern Central America, have spread out southwards to northern Argentina and northwards to the southern border of the USA. Along with such other sub-oscines as manakins and tyrant-flycatchers they are placed in the superfamily Tyrannoidea. The other great sub-oscine assemblage, the woodcreepers, ovenbirds, ant-birds and allied species, are placed in the superfamily Furnarioidea. Though these taxonomic terms may not trip easily off the tongues of the uninitiated, they are of extreme importance in understanding the contribution made by adaptive radiation to diversity.

Both assemblages have arranged themselves according to the feeding opportunities offered by the height variations in the isolated and developing South American forests. The tyrannoids concentrated on the canopy and the middle layers, whilst the furnarioids came to dominate the trunks and large branches, the lower layers and the ground beneath.

The tyrant flycatchers developed from an ability to catch insects on the wing, in contrast to the woodcreepers that took bark insects and the ant-birds that took anything disturbed by the columns of ants marching across the forest floor.

Manakins and cotingas are frugivorous, the manakins arising from an ability to take smaller fruits, leaving the larger fruits for the cotingas. The uprise of the Andes in time created, as we have seen, a wide variety of new habitats, and new plants with new fruits evolved to suit the new conditions. But it was the cotingas that radiated to exploit the fruits of these sub-tropical and temperate habitats, and it is interesting to speculate that this development may be related to fruit size.

Hummingbirds, Heliconias and isolating mechanisms

The evolution of hummingbirds presents us with a perfect example of adaptive radiation, in terms not only of the number and variety of genera and species, but also of the niches which they are uniquely adapted to exploit.

If we accept the theory that they have evolved from swiftlike ancestors, it is likely that the ancestral hummingbirds fed on insects. These they would most likely have found in close proximity to flowers, and this could have given rise to the nectar-feeding habit, even though many hummingbird species still take some insects as part of their diet.

Hummingbirds are characterized by an energy-rich nectar diet, and by a combination of powerful flight muscles and wing structure that allows unique flight techniques. But it is a matter of chicken-and-egg complexity to speculate which came first, the powerful flight muscles or the energy-rich nectar diet necessary to power them.

Hummingbirds do compete for nectar with some insects, mainly bees and moths; but many flower species, over the period of evolutionary time, have shifted their preferred agent of pollination to hummingbirds away from insects. The inevitable conclusion is that some flowers find pollination by the newer hummingbirds to be more efficient than that by the older insects (these words only referring to the comparative points along the evolutionary continuum at which insects and hummingbirds appeared.)

The proactive part in this process played by flowers sheds new light on the concept of parallel evolution. This not only shows us the process of adaptive radiation at work, but also explains how such a unique species as the White-tipped sicklebill could have evolved to exploit flowers with strongly decurved corollas, Heliconias for example, that are unavailable to other pollinators.

But to see the entire process of Heliconia/hummingbird interdependence we must probe still deeper, and in so doing reveal yet one more eternal biological fact relating to speciation and hence to diversity. The White-tipped sicklebill is just one hummingbird species, but its name derives from an extreme adaptation and one that facilitates field identification. Within the Trochilidae the Hermit hummingbirds are characterized by drabber colours and bills that are merely down-curved, not bent into a sickle shape.

But just as there is more than one species of Hermit so is there more than one species of Heliconia, and all attract hummingbirds with their abundant nectar. In order to avoid the risk of hybridization, Heliconias need an isolating mechanism that will control the pollinating activities of the hummingbirds. They have solved their problem by evolving flower parts of different lengths. In this way, pollen is deposited on a particular part of the hummingbird's body, and is in turn placed exclusively on the stigmas of flowers of the same length, that is to say only on flowers of the same species.

Isolating mechanisms — processes whereby the integrity of each individual species is maintained — are more familiar to birdwatchers in terms of songs, plumages and courtship rituals that are unique to particular species. Yet to examine so precise and complex a mechanism as the mutual dependence of Hummingbirds and Heliconias is to open a window onto a fuller understanding of diversity.

A word of warning — and of encouragement

A visit to the Neotropics is likely to overwhelm the first-time visitor, but it is possible to come to terms with its diversity by following the good advice that was given to me prior to my first visit. "Don't expect the diversity to be apparent on every branch and twig; and view it in terms of ecological niches and adaptive radiation".

How can ice affect the tropics?

It is often naively assumed that only the higher latitudes were affected by the glaciations of the Pleistocene period, and that throughout that time the tropics enjoyed a stable and constant climate. Studies of the historical development of present land forms and of past patterns of plant distribution suggest that this scenario is very far from the truth; and from them a picture emerges of climatic instability that had a profound and dynamic effect on speciation, diversity and endemism.

It is well known that the Pleistocene glaciations absorbed vast quantities of water into the ice sheets and substantially lowered the sea levels around the world. Concurrent with this, though, was a global reduction of moisture. In the tropics this led to an increase in savannahs at the expense of rain forest, giving rise to the metaphor of an archpelago of forest "islands" in a "sea" of savannah.

These "islands" have been termed refuges because they represent the last available suitable habitat for rain forest species. Because species were sufficiently separated geographically from each other, and from other populations of the same species, it was possible for speciation in the refuges to occur in much the same way as on real islands separated by real sea. Rapid speciation was able to take place because the interglacial periods allowed the refuges to expand and contract, and secondary contact to be made between newly speciated populations.

It is important to note, however, that virtually all the evidence for the theory of refuges is circumstantial, despite many studies that support its hypothesis. This is an area of continuing work, and we can look forward to final confirmation some time in the future.

(As an aside on a species of great interest, a theory was put forward in the 1960s that ancestors of Homo sapiens were driven from the forests onto the savannahs by the dessicating effects of glaciation. In this alien environment an adaptive response to the survival imperative was the development of the big brain, in part to facilitate hunting communication, and this may have been a selection pressure that led to human speech.)

76

Distributed by ice and fire

I want to end this chapter by considering the distributional effect on diversity of land bridges; and we now know that these can be formed not only from the volcanic arc principle of Plate Tectonics, but also by lowered sea levels during periods of glaciation.

For example, in the case of Jamaica, it is thought that many birds arrived by island-hopping from Central America when the lowered sea level revealed islands that are now immersed. Also consider the Wren of Eurasia, which is conspecific with the Winter wren of North America. Being the most northerly of all American wrens it is the obvious candidate for crossing the Bering Strait land bridge to Siberia. Throughout Eurasia there now exist 42 races (subspecies) of Wren ranging as far west as possible, to St Kilda off the west coast of Scotland. Significantly, there is only the one full species, Trogldytes troglodytes, throughout Eurasia and this suggests that it has not been in any of its new locations long enough for any full speciation to have occurred.

By contrast the Central American landbridge is thought to have been completed as long ago as 3-5 million years. Even before it was fully formed and still existed as an archipelago, the more mobile families, such as thrushes and jays, hummingbirds and flycatchers, would have already started the interchange between the great continent to the north and the great continent to the south.

Thus the Chiguanco thrush, an oscine passerine of Laurasian origin, occurs as a resident as far south as western Argentina. Thus the Western wood pewee, a sub-oscine tyrant flycatcher of Gondwanaland origin, occurs well into Alaska; though in common with all the tyrant flycatchers found in North America it retains its Gondwanaland affinities by migrating for the winter back to the south.

When the landbridge was eventually complete it permitted an almost continuous belt of rain forest to stretch from South America to Guatemala, especially along the Caribbean. Along this belt birds from Neotropical forest-dwelling families began to move north, and populated Central America with toucans, cotingas, antbirds and others in a pattern that diminishes from south to north. The species that migrated across the landbridge were subject to the normal adaptive pressures imposed by new circumstances. They slowly evolved into new species and ensure great diversity and high levels of endemism. This phenomenon goes some way to explain the extraordinarily high levels of diversity in Costa Rica.

Silky-flycatchers are an interesting example of the southward distribution. Absent from South America, they reached as far south as Costa Rica, though being restricted there to the highland regions they may well have followed a distribution pattern similar to the Hairy woodpecker. Another example can be seen in the drier Pacific coast of the isthmus that allowed birds to disperse south from similar conditions further north; and many birds of northern Central American origin (for example Turquoise-browed motmot, Elegant trogon and Lesser ground-cuckoo) find their most southerly outpost in Costa Rica's north-west province of Guanacaste.

A land bridge in the making

Birds are still moving north and south through the Central American land bridge. This is a reminder that geology and the processes driven by geology are continuing all the time despite our inability, with our short life span, to appreciate it.

To demonstrate this point we must finally leave the Neotropics and look at Indonesia, the only other area in the world with a level of biodiversity approaching that of the Neotropics. It is revealing to compare the geology of the two areas. Indonesia today appears as a chain of islands of varying size and of demonstrably volcanic origin, linking a great southern continent (Australia) of demonstrably Gondwanaland origin with a great northern continent (Eurasia) of Laurasian origin.

Geologists readily acknowledge that the forces that make Indonesia what it is today are virtually identical to those that created the land bridge of Central America, namely tectonic plates meeting in such a way that subduction zones create arcs of volcanic islands. By a process of extrapolation it is possible to suggest — in a geological context — that in Indonesia today there exists a situation very similar to that which existed in Central America prior to the completion of the land bridge.

The avifauna of Indonesia provides supporting evidence. When Alfred Russel Wallace delineated the boundary between the Oriental Region and the Australasian Region he did so by noting the point at which Asian influences on birds ceased and Australasian influences began. The line separating the two regions, and which bears Wallace's name to this day, runs between the islands of Bali and Lombok, placing Borneo and the Philippines firmly in Asia and the remaining islands of the Lesser Sundas together with New Guinea in Australasia.

Scientists today recognize that Wallace's demarcation may not be as black and white as he suggested, and that his line may not per se separate more than a few species. Furthermore in 1902 it was shown that the line of faunal balance between the two Regions lay further east than Wallace had suggested, and was named Weber's line after the proponent of this theory. (See Fig D)

These two lines bear close examination. For a start they run in startling proximity to the 200 metre marine contours of the region that outline the edges of the respective continental shelves; Wallace's line following the Sunda shelf and Weber's the Sahul. Of more than peripheral interest is the total isolation in which this leaves Sulawesi and which contributes to its phenomemal levels of endemism.

The area between the lines, known to ornithologists as Wallacea, has a direct bearing on the theory of land bridge interchange. With some under-statement, Wallacea has been described as a great mixing ground. Not only has the island effect ensured endemism at both specific and subspe-cific levels; but as Wallace noted and subsequent ornithologists have con-firmed, the area contains an amazing melange of species of both Asian and Australasian origin.

It is my belief that by studying the avifauna of Wallacea we can gain an insight into the mechanics of interchange and species distribution that exist in the Neotropics and which make both areas endlessly fascinating to geologists and ornithologists alike.

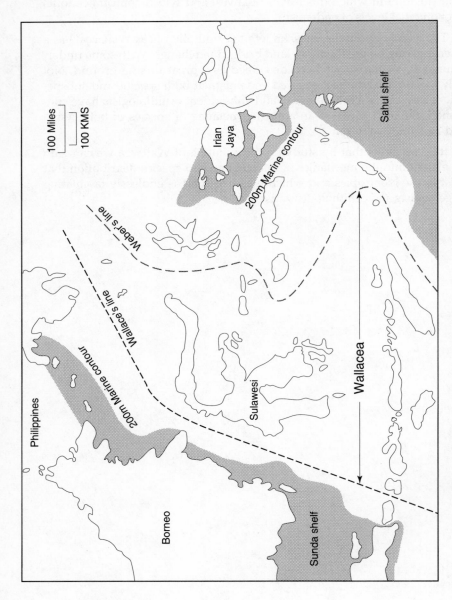

Fig d. Indonesia: illustration of Wallace's line dividing the Oriental Region and the Australasia Region: and the Weber line revising the theory.

PART III

JOY IN DIVERSITY

CHAPTER 9

KOKAKO SONG

Here I am, standing on the Te Kihi track, a rough cross-country road linking Hauturu Road with Kawhia Harbour on the west coast of New Zealand's North Island. The time is 7.20 am, and at approximately 500 metres in the forest on the slopes of Mount Pirongia there is a chill to the air, even though in late November we are well into the austral Spring. Of course I am interested in Mount Pirongia itself, for this is an extinct volcano lying precisely on the margin between the Pacific and Indian tectonic plates.

After a night of rain, hosing in the colourful Kiwi metaphor, the sky is now cloudless, but as yet the sun is only striking the treetops. The forest is montane and as such should bestow some sense of familiarity, but the podocarp and tawa vegetation is, like so much else, unique to New Zealand.

As I wait I catch glimpses through the trees of a sea of emerald green vegetation on the gently contoured slopes of Pirongia Forest Park. As a new-comer to New Zealand I am struck by the proliferation of tree ferns, which I had only previously known from the wrappers of New Zealand butter or the shirts of New Zealand rugby players. I have just learnt, from my friend and guide, Ian Reid, that tree ferns are good species to indicate the purity of native bush; but I have also just learnt that the introduced possum is fast destroying it, and is thus a major factor in the decline of the key endemic forest bird species.

The front that brought yesterday's rain has moved away eastwards into the Pacific, leaving not a vestige of the wind that can make bird watching so frustrating, and giving instead a fresh-washed sky and light of luminous intensity. I have done many dawn choruses over the years and though every one is special this morning's has an air of adventure and mystery about it. The inevitable early start always ensures that I am short of sleep, and this physical condition allows me to view the world through eyes which, though not actually different, seem to have a different perspective. Psychologically, I always feel out of my own element and deep into that of the birds I am hoping to watch, almost that I am in their territory on their terms and by their leave. And in the circadian scheme of things, there is no doubt that I am at that point when night yields to day, a time that links me to the wheeling of the cosmos in ways that no other birdwatching experience can.

Picture me then. On the other side of the world from home. Sleepy, but in that state of heightened awareness and anticipation that pumps the adrenalin, that tightens the nerves and sharpens the senses. The perfect weather, all the more so after yesterday's downpour, with clear sun and still air. The chill of the dawn and the warmth of the coffee. Ears that strain to catch the slightest sound from the forest. The whispered conversations, suddenly broken off at the snapping of a twig. Eyes cast upwards to scan the treetops. The crick in the neck. Waiting, waiting ...

Suddenly, the concentration is shattered — but not the silence. The intruder is a Morepork, the race of Boobook owl endemic to New Zealand's north island. The bird has been sitting — for how long, I wonder? — on the stem of a tree fern sheltered from our sight by the higher fronds; it now glides silently past us and into the forest. I laugh with my companions — softly, of course — to think that it took an owl to remind us that the natural world runs on its own terms, that in the forest it is business as usual regardless of these humans and their quest. The morepork, a new bird for all but Ian Reid, is an interesting bird in its own right, but now scarcely can a new bird have caused so little excitement in a group of birdwatchers.

I settle down to wait again. The light intensifies, moves further down the trees. It can't be long now, can it? How many did you say were in the area?

Then it happens. The song we have all been waiting for begins at last. All dawn birdwatches involve song, but never was there a song like this. I don't really believe it is possible to describe in mere words the song of the Kokako. The books have a go — "the organ music of the forest", "a rich melody of notes", "a double call (short bell-like note followed by a sharp kik.)", and so on. My own vivid imagination leaps at once to a harmonium with a hole in the bellows, tentatively played with one finger by a novice with a penchant for staccato semi-quavers. No, that isn't right either.

One bird starts singing and is shortly answered by another close by, very probably its mate since pairs always feed close together. Others join in till within thirty minutes or so I am able to identify six individuals that are laying down a shimmering blanket of sound over all the forest. And as I listen, entranced, I am strongly reminded of other creatures around the world that use far-carrying dawn songs to enhance their territorial claims; the indri lemur, the howler monkeys, the gibbons — all mammals. To them I now add the Kokako, a bird. How typical of New Zealand.

Kokakos pair for life and may live up to 20 years. Thus there is a strong possibility that the six birds we are hearing are in fact three pairs. In so comparatively small an area this appears at first sight to constitute a reasonably healthy population; yet the alarming fact in New Zealand is that 70% of its native species are endangered, none more so than the Kokako.

In New Zealand, the world's most isolated large landmass, it is perhaps not surprising that so many of its native creatures should be winged, and its only native mammal a bat. Land based mammals, predators and

82

otherwise, were unknown in New Zealand throughout evolutionary time right down to the point of invasion, some thousand years ago, by the people of the Polynesian diaspora who became the Maoris.

The Maoris brought with them their domestic stock, wreaking havoc with the native species and hunting the Moas to extinction. The Europeans who began arriving in the 19th Century brought with them the alien farming methods of empire-building colonists and an environmental ethic not tempered by our late 20th century knowledge and sensibilities.

As I strain my ears to catch the first notes of the Kokako song, I find it peculiar — not to say unnerving — to recognize Blackbird and Chaffinch song within this dawn chorus. These exotic species were introduced by the Acclimatization Societies to make the settlers from the British Isles feel more comfortable in a distant land. This tampering with natural balance would never be countenanced today, but — unwittingly — it has provided laboratory specimens and laboratory conditions for students of population dynamics and population genetics.

Far more serious were the felling of forests for sheep pastures, the dogs, cats, goats and pigs that the settlers brought with them, and the ship rats that inevitably accompanied them on a voyage half way round the world. In the 1860s, in an attempt to establish a fur trade, the Ring-tailed possum was deliberately introduced from Australia; and immediately and gladly filled a previously unoccupied ecological niche. With hindsight we can see that such action would have a catastrophic effect on the native forest, but in the second half of the 19th Century such environmental sensitivities were less finely honed than they are today. Mustelids appeared, maybe originally as pets, and now the stoat is a fearsome predator. More recently and for reasons of agricultural diversification deer were introduced and from time to time escape from their enclosures to join the possums browsing in the forest.

In their research into the decline of the Kokako, the New Zealand Forest Research Institute has identified two distinct factors that have different but cumulatively disastrous effects on the breeding success of the Kokako — browsing and nest predation. Browsers reduce the food supply to the point where Kokakos find it difficult to reach breeding condition. As a result, fewer pairs are attempting to breed, and many that do are failing because of nest predation by ship rats and stoats.

The Forest Research Institute locate nests and observe the outcome. In 1989 they noted, in the tawa forest north of Rotorua, that of six nests located three were predated at the egg stage. Kokakos, as a species, do not nest every year, possibly as a legacy of their longevity and their evolution in a land without predators. The Forest Research Institute also noted that of four pairs in an area only one pair nested that year. That nesting was late in the season and ended in predation.

As if to add weight to their conclusions, the population of Kokakos translocated to Little Barrier Island are thriving in an environment free of browsers and nest predators. In a good cricketing metaphor, this population is currently only looked on as a longstop; yet there may come a time when Kokakos will join Stitchbirds and Saddlebacks as native species that only exist as a result of such proactive conservation methods.

Containment of mainland predators is seen as a more practical option than total eradication, however desirable that might be. As new techniques and materials increase the body of knowledge, many schemes are attempted and evaluated. It has, for example, proved possible to eradicate ship rats from islands up to 180 hectares in size; in fact, manpower is the only limiting factor in a process that involves mapping and baiting all the rat-runs in a given location. And until the use of helicopters was introduced no one had thought it possible to contain escaped deer.

New Zealand is fortunate in its Conservation bodies; the Government funds the Departments of Conservation and of Scientific and Industrial Research, while Non-Governmental Organizations include the Ornithological Society of New Zealand and the Forest and Bird Society. These organizations provide a combination of dedicated research and pragmatic optimism in the fight to ensure a future for the Kokako; and this approach is gratefully reinforced by the presence of this amazing bird in its remaining strongholds.

Meanwhile, back at my chosen stronghold the birds of Mount Pirongia are still singing. What is more, the closest pair has made it to the top of the tree right above my head and this allows me excellent sunlit views; a great improvement on my first view when they had only glided into the lower branches before their painstaking climb to the top.

I am looking at a bird some 15 inches (38 cms) long, with dark bluish-grey plumage, a long tail and short rounded wings conspicuously gapped between the feathers in flight. A broad band of velvety black passes back from the base of the heavy, black, slightly decurved bill, and encircles the eye as a narrow ring. The shiny black legs are long and powerful, and bear identifying plastic rings, from which the conservation bodies can identify and locate every single bird. But the Kokako's most conspicuous feature is the pair of cobalt blue wattles hanging down on either side of the bill. The Kokako, along with the Saddleback and the extinct Huia, form the family of New Zealand wattlebirds, and Wattled Crow is the Kokako's alternative name.

These anatomical details prepare me for its behaviour, form being determined by function in a process with which I am by now familiar. The rounded wings seem incapable of much sustained flight; indeed its maximum distance is only 20 to 30 metres, and it seems to prefer gliding, as with such "downhill" flights as from the top of one tree to the lower branches of the next. This, and its habit of clambering about in the trees, leads some observers to see the kokako as a kind of avian flying squirrel, whose ecological niche in a squirrel-free environment it appears to inhabit.

The size of the bill is determined by its winter diet of tough leaves, whilst the shape is dictated by its fruit and insect diet at other times of year. Its habit of feeding on the best available seasonal diet marks it down as an omnivore, a generalist by David Lack's definition, and one that has had many millions of years in which to adapt to island dwelling.

Right now, the kokako pair that I am watching, complete their serenade on my nearest treetop. They fly then glide, the one closely following the other, to a lower point in a tree across the Te Kihi Track and lower down the slope. They proceed to clamber slowly to the top of that tree, feeding as they go, till they reach the full sun at the top. Here they continue their song where they left off.

The unearthly song and strange primitive appearance of the Kokako have a profound emotional effect on all who share the experience. Jessica Holm, recounting her experiences of Kokako watching on the BBC's Natural History Programme, was moved to liken the experience to listening to a bird that is already extinct, of hearing the last verse of an ancient poem being recited to a fast-emptying forest. This feeling of desolation is compounded and returned to the realms of scientific objectivity by knowing of the Kokako's highly endangered status and that of its fragile forest habitat. I cannot but applaud the research and conservation work that is being carried out to protect both.

Work of this kind is carried out for a variety of reasons, not least for the contention that man has no moral right to allow the extinction of any species. Of all the birds which have become extinct in the last hundred years almost 90% have been island species; and the main causes have been the alteration to native vegetation and the introduction of alien species. New Zealand is a good and obvious place to consider the relationship between island endemism and the incidence of island extinctions.

The isolated geographical location of New Zealand and its early breakoff from Gondwanaland have ensured an exceptionally high level of endemism descended from very ancient stock indeed. No study of endemism can ignore the island effect or the role that New Zealand has played in our understanding of either phenomenon. The Kokako serves as a good symbol of both and one on which we can pin our hopes for a future of better understanding.

CHAPTER 10

JUST DESERTS

Cartoon time in Arizona

I wake early and draw back the curtain in the cabover. I am not yet accustomed to sleeping in this cramped space over the driver's cab of our rented RV, recreational vehicle, camper van — call it what you like; but have to admit that it is an ideal means of transport and accommodation in a country where the spaces are wide and open.

August in Arizona is not exactly busy, though the people I see on the Interstate Highways appear to be constantly on the move and could prove me wrong. For August in Arizona is hot; hot for the visiting English on a summer holiday imposed by the tyranny of school term dates; hot, too, for Americans and Canadians who live in those parts of this huge continent where it is also hot in August.

This explains why I look out of my window over acres of empty RV park where only three of its 2,000 spaces are occupied. Come back in the Christmas high season, when the temperature is a cold 75 degrees; then the park will be full of vans, bearing plates from Minnesota, North Dakota, Wisconsin, Ohio, Manitoba ... their owners only too glad to escape to the warmth of this southern desert.

Today, thankfully, the three RVs are not bunched together but widely scattered over this huge expanse. The intervening space is totally empty. Or is it? As I watch, a creature runs busily across, crested head held forward on a long neck, tail held out as a balance-weight behind it. Suddenly it stops dead, the tail cocks up, the neck cocks up and the head rotates from side to side like the periscope of a submarine scanning the horizon for destroyers. Evidently, it finds none. The neck goes down, the tail goes down and the whole process is repeated. This is a bird, and such an amusing bird that I laugh outright, and wake my wife.

The Hollywood cartoon industry leans heavily on the natural world for its inspiration; rabbits, bears, ducks, mice, coyotes, all involved in activities of catastrophic improbability. But one cartoon character is represented accurately. I know. It's the one I'm watching from the cabover window. All that's missing is the "Beep beep!" For I am watching a Roadrunner, a bird of such amusing and engaging habits that I am astonished that it was not the first creature ever to find its way onto cartoon celluloid. Where all the other characters have human personalities tacked onto them, Roadrunner is left as its own crazy natural self.

Let us exchange this whimsical anthropomorphism for ornithological fact. The species in Arizona is in fact the Greater Roadrunner, which occurs from the southern USA to south central Mexico. Its sole congener, the Lesser Roadrunner, occurs in Mexico and the northern part of Central America. Together they form the genus Geococcyx, and are the best known of the thirteen species of ground-cuckoos found exclusively in the Americas.

Roadrunners feed largely on small snakes and lizards. They kill them by pounding them with their heavy bills, then swallow them head first; and it is these prey items that they are seeking with their periscope head action. Their fastest running speed has been timed at 23 miles per hour, but they are weak fliers and generally sedentary. Their song is described as a dovelike cooing, descending in pitch; though my own preference is for a distant howling dog.

Roadrunners possess a bare patch of black skin on their backs, which in behaviour reminiscent of some reptiles they expose to the early morning sun as a means of quickly absorbing heat for the new day. In so hot a place as the Arizona desert heat dispersal would seem to be more of a problem; and incubating Roadrunners have been observed panting, a common avian practice for reducing body temperature. Nesting activities are in fact the only occasions when Roadrunners prefer wings to legs. They have to fly up to their nests which they make in cactus plants, thus demonstrating a neat adaptation to desert living by using cactus spines as a natural defence against nest predators.

To all this study of Roadrunners there are two predictable responses by English birdwatchers. One is to marvel that any cuckoo builds its own nest and incubates its own eggs. The other is to note that its call is not the familiar "cuckoo". Here perhaps is a lesson in practical avian diversity, the result of travel experiences. Fundamental anatomical and morphological similarities delineate the family; but within the family there are such specific differences as the habit of brood-parasitism and a rich variety of calls. What does seem obvious is that the family was named by people whose first familiarity was with the Common cuckoo and its eponymous call.

Later that same day I drive the RV along a rough desert road, with great care because of the road surface and my own unfamiliarity with the rented vehicle. Keeping pace with me just in front is a Roadrunner running in the desert. At no point does it take to the air, nor does it turn off into the desert scrub on either side of the track; a remarkable and innate response to this intrusion by humans into its environment, not unlike the near contempt with which I was treated by the Brown kiwi in Waitangi Forest.

The Sonoran Desert of Southern Arizona is an extraordinary and unique environment, to which birds and other creatures are well adapted. The situation is the exact reverse of the Atacama Desert of Peru. The Sonoran Desert occurs on the landward side of coastal mountains, the essential difference from Peru being the absence of a strong cold coastal current. The prevailing winds in the southwestern USA are westerly, bringing in moisture-laden air from the Pacific. This is forced upwards by the coastal mountain ranges and lost as rain at the higher altitudes, creating conditions to the east that come closest to true desert anywhere in North America. I recall that on the Roadrunner day the noon temperature at the Arizona Sonora Desert Museum was 110 degrees Farenheit, with 10% humidity.

In the Sonoran desert there is a great number and variety of plant species. The great Saguaro cactus, the "trees" of the desert, cover the floor and the rocky slopes, but they are only one of some six or seven cactus species found here in abundance. Moreover there are scores of other flowering plants that only wait for the infrequent rains before flowering and setting seed. These seeds, and the insects attracted to the plants that produce them, form the basis of a complex ecosystem where there exists a surprising number of birds.

The trouble with sparrows . . .

The rains tend to come in July, as was the case in the year of my visit; and in August the desert is full of flowers and singing birds. This is not the first image that springs to mind at the mention of the word "desert", nor is the image of a sparrow singing as beautifully and as characteristically as any warbler.

Ornithological travellers on their first visit to North America quickly run into the "sparrow problem". Instead of the familiar House sparrow and increasingly less familiar Tree sparrow, both of the genus Passer within the Family Ploceidae (sparrows and weavers); they are confronted by an index with 36 species all bearing the name sparrow (and many others bearing less obviouly helpful names, like Towhee and Junco) from a wide range of genera within the Family Emberizidae. These they know more readily as Buntings. So, putting it all down to experience and nomenclature, they set out — again! — to learn a bewildering array of little brown jobs.

At the desert edges the dividing line is vague and blurred between habitat that can be classified as desert and that which cannot. It is generally marked by the growth of mesquite, a prickly leguminious shrub, and this is especially true in the vicinity of watercourses which, by August, are again nearly dry and earn the Spanish name arroyo. Here, too, at the desert edge are the RV parks, and here itinerant birdwatchers can put down temporary roots. Out come the binoculars and it doesn't take me too long to locate the imitation warbler singing in the mesquite bush.

Of course it's a sparrow; and the song is rapid and high pitched with a trill following two clear notes. So far so good. It has a large and distinctive triangular black patch on throat and breast in contrast to white on eyestripe, moustachial stripe and underparts, and these features resolve it easily into the aptly-named Black-throated sparrow. My field guide shows it to be resident in southern Arizona and fairly common in the desert.

Buntings are seedeaters, and the sighting of this sparrow in such close proximity to the mesquite gives the necessary clue to its diet and hence its survival in the desert.

A brilliant cloak

It soon becomes clear that southern Arizona is a wonderland of birds, many of which occur nowhere else in the USA. So it is that many of the Arizona birds are as unfamiliar to most American birdwatchers as they are to the visiting English, and are highly prized by us both. Yet from this array one bird seems to stand out; partly for its rarity value, partly for its striking appearance, but mostly for its name — Phainopepla.

Initially, such a splendid name take us all by surprise, but spoken slowly and phonetically it can soon become almost pronounceable. To those with a smattering of Greek the words "brilliant" and "cloak" spring to mind; and indeed the male is resplendent in black shining plumage, set off by a long tail, prominent crest and diagnostic grey wing patches.

The Phainopepla is the most northerly representative of the family of Silky-flycatchers, to which I have already referred; yet it is still restricted in the USA to the arid southwest. The family penetrates south as far as western Panama, and then only as specialists in highland habitats. All this points to a Central American origin and to some very precise niche adaption. Silky flycatchers are closely related to Waxwings which they generally resemble in size, but the Phainopepla is the only member of its family to lack a common name. This smacks of inconsistency, and maybe a little mischief, on the part of those same nomenclatural authorities who perpetrate such banal names as "Eye-ringed flatbill" and "Dullmantled antbird."

Names, families, identification, even genetic orientation — none of these seem of such great importance when compared to the thrill and surge of joy that I feel while watching these strange and graceful birds flycatching in the hot Arizona sun. While I am watching I am joined by two birdwatchers from New York. They, too, are watching Phainopeplas for the first time, and this is not so surprising really, given the huge size of North America and the myriad niches to which birds have adapted. Their state of excitement is similar to mine, and this excitement is a powerful bonding agent. Not for the first time, I am struck by the power of birdwatching to form and maintain lasting friendships; and I have an address book that is copiously annotated with places and species alongside names and addresses.

Phoebe Snetsinger

I have a very special place in my address book, and in my heart, for Phoebe. How was I to know that this softly-spoken American lady, with whom I watched birds in Israel, holds the Ladies' World Record life list? Two years after Israel she saw her 7,000th bird — Ceylon frogmouth. And how was I to know that she had used birdwatching to gain for herself at least twelve years remission from a malignant melanoma? Phoebe is the stuff of legend, and by her persistence and dedication shows those of us who follow behind that it can be done!

Another time, another desert

Yet Phoebe is just as anxious as I am to find Sinai rosefinch at Ein Netafim. This species occurs in four races from northwest China through to the Sinai peninsular where one race is endemic. Phoebe shares my pleasure and relief when at last they appear, though we are both underwhelmed by these drab and ordinary birds — females, of course. The males in breeding plumage are a beautiful pink with a silkywhite cast on crown and ear coverts but, in the way of all good birdwatching, they will have to wait till next time.

The word "Ein" (or "En") is a Roman transliteration of the Hebrew word for "spring", and its widespread use as a prefix in place names — En Gedi, for example — points to the life-saving importance of water in the desert.

The road to Ein Netafim from the resort of Eilat, the most southerly point of Israel, follows the so-called Moon Valley — look no further to infer its barren starkness. The place is a Biblical wilderness of rocks and mountain walls, where a great cliff blocks the end of a deep *wadi*, the Arabic word for *arroyo*. There is no doubt in my mind that this strange topography was formed by water in a period of somewhat different climate; the cliff is so obviously a dried-up Niagara, and the *wadi* a dried-up river valley. As if in proof there is, at the foot of the cliff, a tiny spring barely capable of filling a small drinking trough. Oasis it is not, but in this wilderness any water holds the key to the wildlife riches of the area.

For rich it certainly and amazingly is. Most noticeable is the flock of noisy and inquisitive Tristrams' starlings. (Canon Tristram was a 19th Century English clergyman who was sent to the Middle East for the good of his health and proceeded to watch and name a number of local birds.) Though not endemic by the 50,000 square kilometer criterion, the range of Tristram's starling is restricted to the coastal strip of Saudi Arabia and Yemen, the Sinai peninsular and inland desert Israel. They are glossy black with bright rusty primaries that flash brilliantly in flight; but their most engaging characteristic is an arresting wolf-whistle call.

In this rocky amphitheatre calls, especially whistles, echo and reverberate till their origin becomes confused and imprecise. But calls testify to the presence of wildlife, and after much searching we trace other and very different whistles to a small group of Rock hyrax, the coneys of the Bible and closest living relatives of elephants, a relationship difficult to infer from their small almost rodent-like appearance.

Convergent evolution at the Pumping Station

The creation of a tourist resort in so hot and barren a location as Eilat has involved the inventive Israelis in the task of pumping and purifying water for the tourists' use. As part of this complex infrastructure there is a pumping station in the hills above the town. Located in a barren valley, it is an unlikely setting for birdwatching; yet, as I have come to expect over the years, birds do not include aesthetic appeal on their list of good habitat criteria. This superficially unprepossessing location is a prime birdwatching site; but the scattering of acacia trees — leguminous relations of the mesquite — with their seeds and their capacity to attract insects is part of the explanation. As always, water holds the key; and at the time of my visit, a tap was kept permanently dripping to allow the birds a small but permanent source of water.

Birdwatchers with an affection for Hummingbirds find the Old World a little frustrating; that is, until they discover Sunbirds. By a process close to convergent evolution, Sunbirds rival Hummingbirds in the diversity of their brilliant iridescent plumage if not precisely in their anatomical specialization. The wings of Hummingbirds are uniquely rigid and lack the "elbow" that permits the wings of other birds to bend. Hummingbird flight is entirely controlled by the shoulder joint, and this is the anatomical factor behind the hovering technique that allows Hummingbirds to reach otherwise inaccessible flowers. It is significant that Sunbirds, with their bending wings, prefer to take even their nectar food from a perched position, though they will take it on the wing, as an exception, if this is the only means of access. Precisely the opposite of the Hummingbird way.

The Sunbird species at the Eilat pumping station is the accurately named Palestine sunbird. The male in breeding plumage is a gorgeous creature; a dark blue-black with iridescent violet-blue on upperparts, breast and forehead, though the orange tufts at the side of the breast which give him his alternative name are difficult to see except at close quarters or in the hand at a ringing station. He sits in his acacia tree trilling his high pitched rambling song to defend his territory and to attract his greyer, drabber mate.

Occasionally he comes to the tap to drink, and here he joins a mixed assemblage of birds all drawn like him by the magic of water; Trumpeter finch, Tristram's serin, Blackstart and White-crowned black wheatear. Occasionally during the day Sand partridge visit the drinking place; and every evening just after sunset a flock of Lichtenstein's sandgrouse fly in from the desert to drink and to disappear in the same mysterious way.

Seven species of Wheatear

Gradually the truth dawns that these deserts are not the barren wastes that popular fiction and ill-informed semi-knowledge might imply, proving again that there is no substitute for practical experience. Diversity here between genera is matched by diversity within genera, and there is no better example than the genus Oenanthe — the wheatears.

Birdwatchers, like me, who learnt their trade in northern Europe, know "the wheatear" as the true harbinger of spring. One of the first migrants to make it back to England for another breeding season, its neat form — common to all the chats — and flashing white rump (the name Wheatear derives from Anglo-Saxon words for "white arse") are a thankful reminder that winter is past. But amid the current (1993) furore over the re-naming of some common birds, a visit to Eilat proves that there is some value in re-naming this bird "Northern wheatear". Not only does it denote its geographical distribution, but it also states its specific status separating it from all the others.

Before the trip to Eilat my familiarity with other wheatear species was patchy. In Malta I had made the acquaintance of the Black-eared wheatear and in 1984, with stunned amazement, I had seen this species again in Snowdonia on one of its rare vagrant visits to the British Isles. On two visits to the rocky Serrania de Ronda in Southern Spain I had found the delightful Black wheatear, but these three are the only species likely to be encountered in Europe. It takes a visit to the deserts of North Africa and the Middle East to appreciate the full flowering of wheatear diversity; and to realize how properly these birds are adapted to arid conditions, even to the extent of needing no more moisture than that which they can derive from dew and from their insect food.

I encounter seven species of wheatear in Israel, yet another good example of adaptive radiation. Three are passing through on migration and four are resident. Of the resident species, three — Mourning, Hooded and White-crowned black — have plumage variations on the theme of black-and-white. These are colours noted for their capacity to absorb and reflect heat, figuring in the adaptive requirements for desert dwelling; and I am reminded of the Roadrunner with its black skin patch for absorbing heat. The three migratory species — Northern, Black-eared and Isabelline — have varying amounts of sandy and apricot tones in their plumage as well as some black, white and grey. The apparently anomalous species

93

that I encounter is the resident Desert wheatear, whose plumage is the most strikingly black and apricot. The species occurs in three races, two of which are migratory and only one — here in Israel — is sedentary. It is interesting to speculate that plumage variation of sandy and apricot might be a migratory adaption; if so, it is likely that the plumage of the Desert wheatear derives from the characteristics of the two migratory races.

■ The lesson of survival

My desert journey has taken me a long way from the RV park in Arizona, not only in terms of geographical distance but also in terms of ornithological understanding. Deserts are precisely defined ecosystems with precisely defined — and demanding — survival requirements. In my experience they are also places of abundant wildlife, wildlife which by many criteria should not survive there at all. The survival imperative is the strongest biological urge of all, and deserts demonstrate how it is possible for creatures to adapt for survival on the very edge of existence.

A visit to tropical rain forest is awesome in its proliferation of species in these ideal conditions for life; but I am tempted to believe that species that cannot adapt to survive in a moist ecosystem of such warmth and plenty cannot adapt to survive anywhere. Wheatears in the desert demonstrate that some birds are made of sterner stuff.

CHAPTER 11

STREAMERTAILS AT BREAKFAST

A tropical time capsule

The Great House is still standing and is still a Great House, one of the last in Jamaica to be used as a private residence. Set in the hills above Mandeville, it was built in the 1780s and originally served as the nucleus of a 4,000 acre plantation devoted to coffee and a little cattle raising. All that now remain of this venture are the ruins of the slave quarters, little more than outlines in a back pasture, the extensive barbecues (flat concrete terraces) around the House on which the coffee beans were laid out to dry in the sun, and the small amount of coffee that the family still grow for domestic consumption, much like in England they might grow runner beans.

The House is built of cutstone and wood. This might seem odd in a tropical country where termites flourish, till you realize that it is built from the aptly-named bullet wood. The ground floor still exhibits traces of its earlier use as a coffee factory, and you can clearly see the track of the great wheel that was used for separating flesh from seed in the process known as chumming. The wheel itself is preserved elsewhere on the Estate.

The chatelain of the House is Arthur Sutton. Now in his nineties and eighth generation Jamaican born, he has a highly developed sense of historical perspective and continuity. Many of the contents of the House reflect Arthur's interests and hobbies, from a small and priceless collection of Arawak artefacts, to antique furniture, shells, stamps and — his late wife having been a noted botanical artist — books on horticulture and botanical paintings. The House features in all good guide books to Jamaica, and for a small fee Arthur will show his treasures to any tourist with sufficient interest to make the journey.

But times have changed, not only in the wider world of Jamaica but also in the time capsule of Great House and Estate. Instead of a 4,000 acre coffee plantation it is today a 300 acre cattle station run by a handful of skilled men. Though Arthur has sold perpheral parcels of land to satisfy some of Mandeville's more pressing housing needs, the nucleus remains to satisfy the needs of the cattle raising operation. As we shall see, this land has an importance far beyond its 300 acres.

Cattle cannot be pastured on concrete, and anyone with environmental sensitivity who would create a viable stock raising operation on the rolling uplands in this part of Jamaica must maintain the necessary pasture land, whilst at the same time retaining blocks of woodland and linking hedgerows. Whether by accident or design, the result is a near perfect environment, that retains much of the original bush of upland Jamaica, and encourages substantial edge or ecotone habitat much favoured by wildlife and those who would watch it. The area is a discreet whole, managed both for residents and visitors of all types, who see in it the conservation ethic in microcosm — a habitat managed both for human and wildlife interests.

The cattle station is run by Arthur Sutton's son, Robert, a noted ornithologist. It comes as no surprise to me to find that I am greatly interested in this genetic quirk, similar to the one in my own family, that changes natural history disciplines between two generations and fashions an ornitholgist out of the son of a botanist. In Robert's case it is difficult to know which activity takes precedence, stock raising or birds, though I suspect that the former is dictated by the head and the latter by the heart.

What is beyond doubt is that no one with a feel for the natural world and raised on this Estate could ignore its richness in bird life and its importance for their protection. Of the 27 endemic species that occur in Jamaica, 20 have been located here; but the checklist for the Estate contains many other species, including resident Caribbean and Greater Antillean birds and many that visit in winter or summer.

The ornithological importance of the estate is recognized by its human visitors as well. David Lack stayed here during the field studies that led to his seminal work, *"Island Biology, illustrated by the land birds of Jamaica"*. Martin Woodcock, the English bird artist, has stayed here, and his delightful cover illustration of the Red-billed streamertail is based on field sketches made in the garden. Richard Holmes, the American environmental biologist, stayed here regularly during his longterm study of New England song birds. By studying Black-throated blue warblers and American redstarts on their Jamaican wintering grounds he was helped to the conclusion that the decline in New England song bird numbers may stem as much from nest parasitism in New England as from destruction or degradation of their wintering habitats.

It is interesting to note that Jamaica is playing a strategic part in a study that will continue to exercise the minds of ornithologists and conservationists, both in the Americas and elsewhere, well into the future. Many believe that there is little to be gained by making this a "North versus South" issue, since there is ample evidence to suggest problems at either end of the migration routes, in New Hampshire just as much as in Jamaica. BirdLife International is currently working with the National Audubon Society in the USA to revitalize the Convention on Nature Protection and Wildlife Preservation in the Western Hemisphere. This little known convention links more than 20 Western Hemisphere nations in efforts to conserve shared resources including, specifically, migratory birds.

The magnetic appeal of the Estate

Richard Holmes, in his studies of warblers and redstarts at the Estate, confirms that knowledgeable birdwatchers from around the world make it their first port of call in Jamaica. Not only can they watch a concentrated selection of Jamaican birds in delightful surroundings, but they can benefit from Robert Sutton's immense knowledge and skilled fieldcraft that quite literally whistles the birds out of the trees. Wintering North American wood warblers all appear — to a novice at least — to call "chip chip", and are not surprisingly known locally as "Chip-chip birds". Every "chip chip" is different yet Robert accurately locates and identifies each species by call.

I have had the good fortune to spend some time at the Estate, and have enjoyed great hospitality from the Suttons. I have tramped their hills by day and by night, and wrestled with problems of song and plumage identification. I have set up mist nets for one of the only regular banding stations in Jamaica. I have attempted — and failed! — to photograph hummingbirds in the garden. I have sat quietly on the patio and marvelled at how many species pass through the garden in the course of a normal day. And I have taken my first faltering steps along the road of birdsong recording, with the intent cooperation of a Sad flycatcher, a bird which in the way of all sub-oscines is no true songster. But my birding experiences in this unique place deserve more space than this random catalogue, and a birdsong recording episode will make a good starting point.

Recording the song of the White-eyed thrush.

Date, 18th March 1992. Time, 5.15 am. Because Jamiaca is in the tropics the hours of daylight and darkness are relatively standard throughout the year. By March the year is beginning to heat up, but at the elevation of Mandeville the temperature only tends to fluctuate between 65 and 85 degrees Farenheit over a 24 hour period. At 5.15 it is pleasantly cool, the moon is still shining from the supine position that always surprises new visitors to the tropics, and there is a faint flush on the eastern horizon presaging (as if we didn't know) another hot day. Birds are waking all around, with a variety of chips, calls and snatches of song.

Yet one bird is pre-eminent, and it is this one that we have risen early to record. To an Englishman the song is noticeably Blackbird-like, and an American would certainly regoznize its similarity to his familiar Robin. We are both right. The bird we are listening to in this Jamaican dawn chorus is the White-eyed thrush, a member of the Turdus genus to which both the American robin and the European blackbird belong.

But stop a minute and consider this. In a continent as huge as North America there occurs only one member of this genus — the American robin, migratory in the northern part of its range. Here in Jamaica, a country smaller than Connecticut and half the size of Wales, there occur two species of Turdus thrush, our present White-eyed thrush and the White-chinned thrush that has a song that is only marginally less beautiful. Both of them are endemic and prove how inevitable it was that David Lack should have considered the mechanics of the island effect in Jamaica.

Our emotions are touched by the beauty of the song which currently absorbs all our attention. Robert, certainly, has known the White-eyed thrush all his life and is still attempting to make the perfect recording. It is only later, when I allow myself the luxury of rational thought, that I am struck by this evidence of those forces that control the spread of new genetic developments and cause endemic species to occur. But I have dealt with this phenomenon elsewhere, and at this point merely prefer to enjoy the emotions aroused by the beauty of the song.

Mainly concerning Potoos.

I never fail to tingle when I share a dawn chorus with the birds. It matters not whether I am watching Blackcaps in an English oak wood or Kokakos among the New Zealand tree ferns — or White-eyed thrushes in Jamaica. It has everything to do with being up and out at a time when our interrupted circadian rhythms heighten the perceptions of all our senses. The same is also true of birdwatching — if that is the right term — at night.

Night birds, and even more so the crepuscular species that are active at dusk, exert a fascination over us that I suspect has more to do with a folk memory of hobgoblins and the faery world than with rational and scientific ornithology. All such birds have wierd and — to some listeners — terrifying calls.

Owls screech in church yards and give rise to tales of ghosts and unquiet souls. The naming of the Kiwi is thought by some to hark back to the ancestral home of the Maoris in Tahiti and Raratonga, where they would have been familiar with the Bristle-thighed curlew, a bird whose call can be rendered as "kivi". This is not remotely similar to the shriek of the Kiwi, but folk memory is notoriously unscientific, and the calls remain to remind the Maoris of the ghosts of their ancestors. English ornithologists are struck by the similarity of the "kee-wick" call common in varying forms to Tawny owl, Woodcock and Nightjar, all birds that are likely to be encountered on the same crepuscular bird watch. And the Nightjar's alternative name of Goatsucker roots it firmly in the English folk memory as a sinister and unwelcome visitor to livestock.

I first arrived at the Sutton's Estate after dark, and was immediately taken by Robert to scan fence posts for Common potoos. His technique is to pick up the red gleam of their yellow eyes in the flashlight beam, and it works.

Found only in the Neotropics, Potoos are Caprimulgiformes and so are closely related to Nightjars, but they differ in their methods of catching their insect prey. Instead of hawking them in continuous flight Potoos hunt in flycatcher fashion, sallying out from a perch to which they return with their catch. For the practical birdwatcher this makes them easier to work; find the perch and you find the Potoo.

Robert continually walks his trails and knows the whereabouts of his Potoos. In a small clearing at the base of a hill behind the Great House there is an obliging dead tree with broken top branches, and to this tree he takes me one evening. We wait. Birdwatchers always wait at dusk and dawn; it gives the adrenalin — and the mosquitos — time to work. But it isn't long before the Potoo obliges. Larger and paler than a European nightjar, it swoops onto its perch, sitting there horizontal and curiously raised fore and aft in its state of feeding alertness. Its distinctive call is best rendered as "Qwaa-a-a-a, qwa-qwa-qwa", which places the Common potoo firmly in the ghosts-of-ancestors league. With this call it sallies out to catch an insect and returns to its perch, leaving the delighted bird-watchers below to wonder to what fearsome beast the original inhabitants attributed its peculiar call.

The ease with which we saw the Potoo and its horizontal pose on the feeding post contrasts vividly with the difficulty of finding the bird at its daytime roost. Potoos roost in a vertical position on broken stubs of branches where their cryptic colouration makes them look for all the world like a continuation of the tree. Try as I might I never found a roosting Potoo in all my day-time searches, despite their obvious frequency on the Estate.

If I have painted a picture of a strange and unusual bird, this was my intent. Yet one disconcerting feature of the Common potoo remains, at least as regards the Common potoos in Jamaica. Ornithologists who have watched the species, mainly in mainland Central and South America, have observed that roosting Common potoos sit bolt upright with their bills pointing to the sky. In Jamaica, however, according to Robert Sutton's painstaking and long-term observations, the Common potoo sits with its head and bill pointing forward at roughly 45 degrees to the body line. This appears to show an anatomical variation which, in the days before DNA-DNA hybridization was used to separate species from species, might have led to speculation that the Jamaican Common potoo ought to be split as a separate species from the one occurring on the mainland. This question is still unresolved.

Streamertails at breakfast.

There is much open air eating in the tropics. Whoever designed the Great House knew his trade and his country, and decreed that the patio should face north. It is always in welcome shade and makes for ideal al fresco meals, particularly breakfast when we join the multitudes of lizards on the edge of the garden.

Suspended on a hook above our heads there is a miniature liqueur bottle half full of the sugar water that hummingbirds demand from their human hosts. As a result our breakfasting is regularly interrupted by the buzzing zip of a hummingbird arriving to feed on this nectar. Not just any old hummingbird, but the amazing Red-billed streamertail.

To describe this attractive little bird I can do no better than to quote from the book that Robert Sutton wrote with his cousin, Audrey Downer: "Head black, lateral crown feathers and ear coverts elongated beyond nape. Body bright iridescent emerald green, darker on back. Wings brown, tail black shot with green, the second to outermost tail feathers very long (13 cm (6 in) or more) forming the 'streamers' which are scalloped and fluted on the inside and create a high whining hum in flight. The streamers are often crossed." Note how a touch of excitement creeps into this factual description, for few observers can retain total objectivity when describing such a bird.

To Old World birdwatchers, lacking any familiarity with hummingbirds, this tiny creature is a total amazement. We are generally unfamiliar with birds that possess inordinately long tails, whatever their size; but a long tail on so minute a bird suspends our disbelief. The garden supports quite reasonable numbers, and they are first identified by the zipping hum of their flight as they trail their tails amongst the lush tropical vegetation.

I have already discussed the processes whereby hummingbirds have spread through the western hemisphere, and have looked in some detail at adaptive radiation and parallel evolution with their food plants; but it is pertinent to state here that the Red-billed streamertail is endemic to Jamaica. Even so, these evolutionary factors hardly explain the extraordinary length of the Streamertail's tail, but this may be as easily explained in terms of courtship display as the puce gorget of Anna's hummingbird and the crests on the Coquettes of Central and South America. But what is beyond doubt is that no other hummingbird, with the possible exception of the two Trainbearers in the Andes, has so resplendent a tail.

The Red-billed streamertail is common in Jamaica, which combined with its startling appearance has placed it firmly in the collective consciousness of the Jamaican people. Not only have they made it their national bird and printed its likeness on their two dollar bill, but they have given it a number of local and affectionate names. The most common of these is Doctorbird, though no one is certain of the reason. Maybe the crossed streamers remind them of the swallowtail coats affected by 19th Century doctors. Maybe the bird's habit of occasionally puncturing the base of the corolla tube to steal the nectar without pollinating the flower reminds them of the doctor's actions when lancing a boil. Maybe, in a country of alternative folk religions, there is a connection in the mind with the Doctor, the Priest of Obiah, the local variety of Voodoo. Who knows? Does it actually matter that much? But in the soporific heat of midday Jamaica such idle speculation is possible without raising a sweat.

Cash crops and foreign exchange earnings

The common occurrance of the Red-billed streamertail, and the affection in which it is held by the ordinary people of Jamaica, takes us away from the secure ornithological confines of the Estate, and gives us an opportunity to view the Estate and its conservation riches in a broader context. A closer look at the environmental pressures affecting Jamaica in general highlight its real value in the wider conservation debate.

In a post-colonial world, we have to face the fact that Jamaica is not a rich country, and the national economy is very much that of a developing nation. Prosperity — both at the national and personal level — is therefore very much dependent on the earning of foreign exchange, and to this objective is much effort devoted. Since the days of the colonial planters the importance to Jamaica of cash crops has been recognized; and it would be interesting to know how many stately homes in England, well stocked with priceless mahogany furniture, are founded on the wealth of Jamaican plantations and the now vanished lowland mahogany forests.

Great swathes of land are devoted to the growing of cash crops, of which bananas, coffee and sugarcane are the most prominent; to which must be added the extraction and refining of bauxite, the ore from which aluminium is obtained. Jamaica is the world's third largest exporter of bauxite; and though it not a "crop" in the same way that coffee is, the bauxite industry has just as great a blighting effect on the environment.

There are, of course, other ways in which Jamaica can earn foreign exchange. Tourism is an obvious and very lucrative invisible earner, and the appeal of the "tropical paradise holiday" is very attractive to hedonistic tavellers, particularly in the depth of the northern winter. Jamaica can boast the whole gamut of exotica — white sandy beaches, clear blue warm seas, palm trees gently swaying in the breeze, good diving and snorkeling, excellent and unusual food and drink ... Some people are so seduced by its appeal that they clamour to be married standing in the warm Caribbean sea.

101

Another factor intrudes itself into the equation, a factor of extreme sensitivity — that of population increase. Jamaica is a country where over fifty per cent of the population is under twenty one, and where a combination of medical techniques and social mores will undoubtedly increase that percentage. Therefore questions need to be asked. Are the cash crops being grown because the national economy demands the foreign exchange from crops at that level? Or are they being grown merely to support the increasing numbers of people who grow them? (If so, it will not be the first time that this has ever happened. For evidence we need look no further than the mountains of unwanted European foodstuffs, grown merely so that farmers shall have a livelihood, at no matter what environmental cost in terms of lost hedgerows and skylarks.) The answers will determine, in large measure, the environmental future of Jamaica — whether, for instance, the principles of set-aside have any future there — as well as Government strategy in such areas as health and family planning.

For this is the Jamaican dilemma, and one that is faced most acutely by its conservationists, none more so than the dedicated staff of the Jamaican Conservation and Development Trust. To maintain and, hopefully, increase the standard of living through cash crop earnings, the quality of the environment has to be sacrificed. If the increasing world demand for coffee, for sugar, for bananas is to be satisfied, how soon will the time come when all suitable terrain for growing such crops is exhausted? And what then? In a tiny remote hamlet in the parish of Trelawney, I have seen sugar cane planted on every available flat surface, encroaching right up to edge of the forest-covered hills. Even on a quick survey of this forest it was possible to identify an astonishing variety of endemic birds, plants, reptiles and amphibians — all of which would be lost to any expansion of the cane fields.

The value of the Estate

It is in the context of this doomsday scenario that the true value to conservation of the Sutton's Estate can be seen. Whilst so much of Jamaica's natural heritage is falling to clearance for a cash crop mentality driven by the tyranny of economic necessity, so the Estate grows in importance as a wildlife refuge and reservoir. Birdwatchers already visit the Estate to sample the old way and to watch twenty out of the twenty seven endemic species, but none of them would wish it ever to become the only place where such birdwatching is possible.

There must come a time when sustainable development becomes the way of life in Jamaica. The examples from Cameroon that I quoted in Chapter 4 show that such a way is possible, especially when local people have to face the stark realities of environmental degradation. But Jamaica is an island, and this symbolically imposes finite limits as much on its resources as on its shoreline — and on the thinking and aspirations of its people.

If ever there was a country where the dynamic of eco-tourism needs to be implemented, Jamaica is that country. Tropical paradise it undoubtedly is, or can be; but the sybaritic behaviour of tourists, who are merely attracted by self-indulgence in its pleasures, is likely to destroy its fundamental attractiveness. Also destroyed will be the fragile coastal ecosystems where the mangroves can contain as many as fifteen species of wintering North American wood warbler in a quarter mile walk. Twenty seven endemic bird species in an island smaller than Connecticut and half the size of Wales — this is of major appeal to the world's travelling birdwatchers. But until it can be demonstrated to the local people that eco-tourism will earn them more revenue than their current inimical cash crop culture, they will have but little incentive to put eco-tourism initiatives in place. Until, that is, it is too late.

CHAPTER 12

MEETING THE PLUMED SERPENT

Throughout this book, a recurring theme — both written and illustrative — has been the Resplendent quetzal, the most beautiful of the trogons; and to this bird travelling birdwatchers have attached something of the mystique of the Holy Grail. With the exception of its appearance — and I do consider it to be the most beautiful bird in the world — ironically the reality in practice is very different.

The Resplendent quetzal is no more or less difficult to find than many other Central American cloud forest species, and a great deal easier than the Bare-necked umbrellabird. Central American cloud forest is a habitat mainly unfamiliar to European birdwatchers and to many of their North American counterparts. It takes time, effort and money to get to Monteverde in Costa Rica, the most accessible Quetzal location in the world; but the same applies to very many other localities for ultimate birdwatching experiences, and Monteverde is much easier to reach than, say, 15,000 feet up Chimborazo (Andean hillstar) or Halmahera (Wallace's standardwing).

I have allowed myself a little poetic licence in the dismissive opening to this chapter, but this is for no other reason that to add emphasis to the spectacular experience of seeing the Resplendent quetzal for the first time. This is no ordinary bird, even to the locals, who greatly cherish it. Despite the widespread Hispanification of the Costa Rican population you often come across people whose features proclaim them to be of almost pure Indian descent. Though geography dictates that they are more likely to be descendants of Maya than of Aztec, they surely act as a repository for ancient pre-Columbian folk memories in which the Resplendent quetzal played a leading, not to say a dominant role. Let me explain.

For a start, it is not easy to find documented instances where birds have changed the course of history. When the Gauls attacked Rome in 390 BC, the garrison on the Capitoline Hill were alerted to their presence by the cackling of the sacred geese, who were thus credited with saving the City. It is well known that carrier pigeons have their uses in time of war, as do canaries as gas-detectors in coal mines; and the domestication of the Red jungle fowl has benefitted mankind in ways comparable only to that of the cow, the horse and the dog. Though of interest, these matters are hardly the stuff of catyclysm.

By comparison, consider the conquest of Mexico by the Spaniards. When the Conquistador, Hernan Cortes, invaded in 1519, the superstitious Aztec Emperor, Montezuma II, refused to take energetic steps to repulse him, preferring to believe that he was the god, Quetzalcoatl, whose return had been long foretold. Thus unwittingly did a bird assist Cortes in his conquest of Mexico, an event that caused the brutal termination of the entire Aztec civilization, and set in train the Spanish imperial adventure.

The process whereby a bird is adopted into the religion of a country, not merely as a bystander but as a central deity, needs some explanation and presupposes a more than unusually charismatic bird. Those who have wondered about the name "quetzal" (or even its pronunciation — say *ketsaal*, emphasis on the second syllable) must assume that the bird was named before the god. The name of the deity, "Quetzalcoatl" derived from two very obvious aspects of the bird's appearance, and incorporate two Nahuatl words — "quetzalli", precious feather, and "coatl", snake. This, very significantly, gave the god his alternative title of The Plumed Serpent, a powerful image well aimed at the requirements of religious veneration.

To Quetzalcoatl were ascribed many divine attributes, some rooted in ordinary daily life, others in religious veneration and attempts to fathom the unfathomable. On the one hand, he is the god of the winds — the northeast trades — who drives the clouds before him and makes moisture descend upon the earth. This concept is very familiar to anyone who has experienced the spray at Monteverde blowing from the cloud cap on the continental divide mountains. Quetzalcoatl thus becomes the deity of the beneficial influence of the air, of medicines and of the healing arts; functions and attributes that also make him the god of fertility. On the other hand, as the morning and evening stars, Quetzalcoatl is the symbol of death and resurrection — death, if you will, in his ultimate expulsion, and resurrection in his longed-for return from beyond the eastern horizon.

Here, of course, are powerful similarities with other religions; most notably with the reincarnation beliefs of Buddhismm, and with the death, resurrection and second coming of Jesus Christ. There are even more astonishing Christian parallels in Quetzalcoatl's association with the cross, symbolic in his case of the four regions on earth from where the four winds come. Through these examples we discover once again how universal are religious fundamentals and the human desire to fathom the unfathomable; but we have to look closer to find substance for the role of a bird in changing the course of history.

According to the legends, Quetzalcoatl was expelled by the god of the night sky, Tezcatlipoca, and this is most probably a reflection of historical fact. In Mexico, the first century of the Toltec civilization (approximately 600-700 AD) was dominated by the Teotihuacan culture with inspired ideals of priestly rule and peaceful conduct. Pressure from northern insurgents precipitated a social and religious revolution, when a military ruling class seized power from the priests. The downfall of the classic theocracy was symbolized in the expulsion of Quetzalcoatl, but the aspirations of his followers were kept alive in the concept of his longed-for second coming.

Imaginative though Homo sapiens has always been, the Plumed Serpent is such a potent image that it is doubtful that anyone could have dreamed it out of nowhere; and it would be interesting to know the processes of thought and action whereby the Plumed Serpent was chosen, ahead of other contenders, as the most charismatic religious symbol. I am obviously not alone in feeling the attraction of the Resplendent quetzal, nor am I the first to dream that so beautiful a bird must have supernatural attributes.

The trogons are typical of what we, in our northern temperate isolation, think tropical birds should look like. The 39 species form a distinct and uniform family and order of quiet, sedate, solitary inhabitants of tropical forests around the world. The Neotropics hold most species with 25; but the three African species and the 11 from the Oriental Realm testify to their interesting and disjunct pan-tropical distribution, curiously at odds with the sedentary nature of all trogons, a subject on which I have already speculated.

The Resplendent Quetzal is one of the largest and most ornate of the trogons. It is resident in highland cloud forests from southern Mexico to Costa Rica and Panama, where two races are recognized, one in southern Mexico and northern Nicaragua, the other in Costa Rica and western Panama. This precise and distinct distribution reflects the physical geography of Central America, and lends support to the theory of refuges.

In breeding males four of the upper tail coverts grow into long, shimmering green plumes, the two central ones trailing gracefully two feet behind the tail. When it flies towards you it looks like a bird with wings spread wide and a long tail streaming. *When it flies across your front it looks like a flying snake, a plumed serpent.* Thus is scientific anatomical fact linked at last and for ever with charismatic religious experience; and Twentieth Century observers can share the mystical wonder of a beautiful bird with their predecessors down the centuries who created of this creature the pinnacle of their Pantheon.

This sense of wonder has even permeated to the common naming of this bird. Ornithologists, guilty of so boring a name as "Black greybird", are moved to name this bird the *Resplendent* quetzal. The Oxford English Dictionary defines "resplendent" as *"Shining, brilliant, splendid; to be radiant, to shine brightly . . . brilliance, lustre, splendour."* The choice of epithet by the ornithologists is an uncharacteristically subjective, if not a downright emotional response — such is the way with this bird.

Few pictorial representations of the Resplendent quetzal correctly capture its colours. This may have something to do with the exceptionally thin, tender skins of all trogons, which makes them the most difficult of all birds to prepare as museum specimens. So it may be that Quetzal illustrations made from prepared skins are unwittingly based on innaccuracies.

107

This inability of accurate representation is comparable to the inability of live Quetzals to survive long in captivity, and adds to the mystique of a bird which patriotic Guatemalans regard as symbolizing the spirit of freedom.

As with all sedate, sedentary trogons, the Resplendent quetzal is much given to sitting still, sometimes for as long as an hour, in the tall cloud forest trees to digest its cropful of wild avocados, and to eject the pits. In this way, it allows itself to be examined at leisure. Field guides give its body length as 14 inches (36 cms), plus 25 inches (64 cms) for the male's tail streamers. From ground level, where most observers are situated, these dimensions seem a trifle understated. It has a standard length trogon tail which is white underneath, but it is doubtful that many observers will even notice it. Look at the tail coverts — indeed it is difficult to look at anything else! These long, attenuated streamers narrow to a point at the end of their 25 inch length, and present a delicate filligree tracery which sways in the almost constant wind. Indeed, it is this tell-tale movement that is often the first indication of the bird's presence.

Alexander Skutch, the ornithologist and long-time resident of Costa Rica, has written movingly on the subject of light as the essential medium of visual perception. The factors affecting the quality of light in the Quetzal's cloud forest home therefore affect our perception of the Quetzal itself. At 10 degrees north of the equator the angle at which sunlight strikes the earth is less acute than at the higher latitudes with which most birdwatchers are more familiar, and this requires some adjustment. By definition, cloud forest occurs at high elevations and, as is implicit in the name, sunlight is ofen diffused into rainbows or obliterated altogether by the presence of cloud and blowing spray. The distant canopy — some trees can reach 150 feet — strains the sunlight from a great height, and this dappling is further confused by the riotous assemblage of epiphytes, lianas, strangler figs and understorey tangle. Add to this the physical discomfort of watching a bird for an hour through binoculars at an angle of 75 degrees and at a distance of, say, 200 feet (pace Pythagogas), and it is easy to see how colours, dimensions and shapes become distorted and pictorial representation inaccurate.

My field notes dictated at the time of observation reveal the breast of the male as a bright plum crimson; the mantle and wings a bright slaty turquoise shot through with emerald; the head with its shaggy ragged crest apparently almost black; the bill a prominent yellow; and the amazing tail coverts again slaty turquoise shot through with emerald, like the wings and mantle. My companions immediately corroborated this description of the colours and it is crucial that they did so.

I have never seen Quetzals represented in painting or photograph in precisely these colours; even in the excellent and widely available photographs by Mike Fogden, who lives at Monteverde and has apparently photographed Quetzals from the horizontal, the red appears more as scarlet and the green as bright apple. This may have as much to do with the quality of film emulsions (or paint pigments and printing technology, for that matter) as with the physical and emotional conditions under which a person observes the bird. How can photographers portray reverence? How can artists portray a crick in the neck? Should they, in fact, be allowed to try? Or, in deference to the diety, should they veil their eyes and delicately decline?

My enjoyment of birdwatching, especially in remote and wonderful places, has been greatly enhanced by a quotation from Lawrence Durrell's *"Alexandria Quartet"* that man is only an extension of the spirit of place. People whose religious perceptions are simple, unstructured and essentially animist in nature, will already be susceptible to the spririt of place; and will understand how difficult it is to separate wonder at the Quetzal from wonder at its cloud forest home.

The cloud forest ecosystem is unfamiliar to many people, remote and difficult of access, the goal of pilgrimage. Species diversity in cloud forest is overwhelming, the height and structure of the trees truly inspiring and greatly enhanced by the epiphytes, the butress roots and the strangler figs. This forest is primary, untouched, mystical, life-enhancing, life-renewing, reverential. And here in the cloud forest, in its rightful home, sits the Resplendent quetzal, a beautiful bird worshipped as Quetzalcoatl, the Plumed Serpent and god of the winds who drives the clouds before him and makes moisture descend upon the earth; a deity whose eagerly awaited return allowed the Spaniards to conquer Central America and change the course of history. And in a process that satisfactorily completes the cyclical sequence, it is appropriate that the modern day Costa Rican descendants of those Conquistadores should continue to treasure and cherish their Plumed Serpents, to the pleasure of ornithologist and acolyte alike.

EPILOGUE

FAREWELL AND HAIL!

Mountains, mountains, mountains.

From the Psalmist who wrote *"I will lift up mine eyes unto the hills"* to the weary alpinist trudging back across the Mer de Glace after climbing the Aiguille Verte, people have tried to explain the fascination of mountains. Some of their explanations ring true, others false. They range from lightheadedness brought on by high altitude oxygen depletion, to euphoria induced by negatively-charged ions in the atmosphere. They include a feeling of minuteness and insignificance in the face of huge natural forces, akin to that experienced on a night of stars in an incandescent heaven; and a feeling of grandeur and omnipotence emanating from the greatly enlarged vistas and horizons afforded by a high altitude view point. The ultimate paradox of mountains, however, is that this feeling is automatically dissipated by the act of returning to sea level.

Small wonder then that there persists in the human mind the image of the Bhuddist hermit sitting on a Himalayan peak, an image fleshed out by Peter Mathiessen in his book *The Snow Leopard*. He writes of his actual meeting with an aged monk at a high altitude Himalayan monastery, and it comes as no surprise to read that Mathiessen is preoccupied with thoughts of Zen in such surroundings and with such inspiration. Altitude can give rise to deep thoughts of infallibility, and the monk's dictum that "no snowflake ever falls in the wrong place" haunts me to this day.

All lovers of mountains have their favourite mountain and their favourite mountain experience. To Londoners driving to Snowdonia the sight of Moel Siabod looming gradually clearer and larger as they near Betws-y-Coed raises their spirits and reassures them that the long drive is nearly over. An overnight train journey to Switzerland affords a sudden surge of elation as the couchette blind is raised and the incomparable Alps come blazing in. Lone snow-capped volcanoes, like Mount Fuji or Mount Hood, powerfully affect poet and artist alike; and sunset on Annapurna has been known to make strong men weep.

My own encounters with grand mountains are varied — the Jungfrau on a childhood holiday and the Matterhorn in later life; a turbulent Mount Etna seen from the flight-deck of a Boeing 737; Mount Edith Cavell in the Canadian Rockies with its diagonally folded rock strata; Mount Robson towering above the roof of Canada, its icy pinnacle a mirror image of that other pinnacle above Zermatt; Volcan Arenal in Costa Rica, the world's most active volcano, throwing out its glowing lava and raising the dead four times a night with sleep-rending explosions. A strange collection, really, but such is the way of personal experience.

One encounter I hold more dear than any other. In the French Alps of the Haute Savoie I take a cable car from Saint-Gervais to Mont d'Arbois, a 1,827m hill on the edge of the Préalpes, and as I set off there is cloud

111

above 1,000 metres. This is the essence of my tale, which converts it from a tourist excursion into a mystical experience.

At the top cable station I find a seat, and upon that seat I sit down, to face nothing but a thick blanket of cloud. But as I wait the clouds begin to part, fragment, lift and blow away. Little by little across the Val Montjoie there is revealed the glory of the whole Mont Blanc massif, for it is the Val Montjoie that marks the border between the Prealpes and the Real Alps, the eaves of the roof of Europe.

At first there are only the smallest of tantalizing glimpses, a rocky outcrop here, a smudge of glacier there; but as the wind from the valley grows stronger so the curtains part wider and the Domes de Miage come into view. Soon the wind is really rolling up the curtain of cloud, and the Domes du Gouter stand proud, to be quickly followed — where is the fanfare? — by Mont Blanc itself, a veritable Deus ex Machina through whom all things are possible.

Now I begin to understand the exultation with which Richard Strauss wrote the "Auf dem Gipfel" (At the Summit) section of his Alpine Symphony, and why he followed it with a section marked "Vision". He must have felt compelled to write softer music to express his awe at the mighty spectacle and to pour out his admiration in the climax to the whole work. I, too, am overcome.

Meanwhile, the wind continues to blow and the clouds to disperse. Soon I can observe that point, of interest to geologists and mountaineers alike, where the peaks of the Massif change from Domes to Aiguilles (needles) as they march eastwards into Switzerland. Here at last is the Aiguille du Midi thrusting upwards in its terrifying and stark angularity to lance the boil of clouds. Then, with the clouds gone, infinity takes over, and the show moves on. Dynamic change is replaced by the serenity of contemplation.

Gazing along this superlative massif I experience a feeling of euphoria. I am all-powerful, all-knowing, and at the same time — another paradox — minutely humble. I begin to ponder the imponderable. Who am I? What am I doing here? Why is anyone here? And then it happens. At this pivotal point a small flock of Ravens fly tumbling and croaking across the valley, and my questioning abruptly changes course and finds its focus — "What are these birds doing here?"

The genes, first and last.

It is as good a question as any, a gut response to an imponderable question. Goethe had his say when he wrote that the greatest happiness of the thinking man is to fathom that which can be fathomed, and quietly to reverence that which is unfathomable; but as with all "good quotes" this one leaves a lot unfinished. Goethe always thought more in terms of metaphysics than of science, but even so I cannot dismiss him out of hand; he was, after all, a representative of the eighteenth century "Enlightenment" that helped to create the climate in which the likes of Darwin and Wallace could promulgate their theories.

We are luckier than Goethe by having a third choice. We can choose the path of investigation — scientific, philosophical, practical, theoretical — and not deviate until we reach a conclusion. What, I wonder, would have been the outcome if Crick or Rutherford had followed Goethe's advice? So, as we approach the final pages of this book, let us apply this methodology to the question *"Why are these birds here?"*

Being human we are inclined to address the question from the human standpoint. In our blinkered state we compare the successes and failures of the natural world exclusively with our own as if we were somehow separated from it by the birthright concept of Biblical dominance, to which I have referred elsewhere. So to answer the question *"Why are these birds here?"* it might be easier to start by considering why birds are not here.

One thing is certain; birds are not here to give pleasure to humans, either in terms of full bellies or full life-lists, or even full employment for university ornithologists. Birds are not designed to give us aesthetic pleasure in any way, neither from the colours of their plumage nor the beauty of their songs, nor even from the multitudinous diversity of either. They are not designed to impress us with the intricacy of their nest building nor their majestic use of thermals for soaring; neither to inspire poets nor yet to disperse the workaday stress of the jaded weekend birdwatcher. That we do derive benefits — especially emotional and intellectual benefits — from birds at all is far more a big-brain response to the eternal search for the meaning of life than it is any part of the evolutionary process.

As we grope our way along the path of investigation, rejecting all that is negative or fanciful, it begins to dawn on us that birds are at their most alluring during courtship and breeding. It doesn't matter whether we are watching the butterfly display of a Greenfinch in Hertfordshire or the electronic effusions of a Blue Bird of Paradise in Papua New Guinea; a large ragged Osprey nest at Loch Garten or the coinsized nest of a Vervain hummingbird in Jamaica; a Nightingale or a Musician wren or a New Zealand Bellbird. We respond by finding display and nesting activity so riveting because that is when the birds are at their most attractive and energetic. With our perverse logic, and our penchant for anthropomorphism, we have hit on the right answer, but for the wrong reason.

We reach our destination on the path of investigation when we realize that each and every feature of bird activity has but one purpose. The

113

answer to the question *"Why are birds here?"* is quite simple. It is — "Survival, and the passing on of the genes to the next generation." There is no other reason for birds to exist, or for elephants, or for Poplar hawk-moths, or for dandelions — or for us to exist. This dreadful thought may dent our pre-Darwinian egos, may sit ill with our material acquistitive-ness and our self-styled superiority; but we at our level, just like birds at theirs, have this one common objective.

An antidote to pessimism.

As I sit watching the Ravens I am left feeling strangely sad that my question has so material and scientific an answer. Can it really be true that birds exist merely to pass on their genes to the next generation? There must be more to it than that, or am I in my own way merely articulating yet again this yearning for an answer to the meaning of life? Ever the opti-mist, I start looking for another answer — any other answer.

For a start, what if anything do the ravens feel as they go about the business of passing on their genes? In my anxiety I take comfort and strength from a passage written by the incomparable Alexander Skutch in his book *The Imperative Call*:

> *My continuing ignorance of the psychic quality or inner life of the creatures around me, of their true nature, makes me reluctant to harm even the least of them. When we kill any living thing we do not know what we destroy. Birds, for example, seem to live more intensely than we do; their vital processes are more rapid, their senses keener, their reactions swifter; it may also be that they feel more deeply than we do. Although the lifespan of the smaller birds is much shorter than ours, they may crowd more real living into a day than we do into a week or a month. Their relatively uncompli-cated lives amid trees and flowers and sunshine may be more joy-ous and satisfying than ours in a complex artificial world beset with perplexities and misgivings. They may know intuitively much that we try to discover by the slow analytic methods of science, as when without charts or instruments, they find their way to a defi-nite goal over vast expanses of the earth's surface. In short, their lives may be, in various aspects, more perfect than our own, and who would want to be guilty of destroying something more perfect than himself? Even to suspect that the earth supports many crea-tures who live joyously gives us greater confidence that the world process (of which organic evolution is a phase) has not gone miser-ably astray, and is an antidote to pessimism.*

Does this beautiful prose contain my answer? Maybe, maybe not, but it lifts my spirits anyway.

Mass extinction and human interference.

Who, indeed, would want to be guilty of destroying something more perfect than himself? From the fossil record it has been possible to calculate that bird species reached a peak of some 11,500 during the Pleistocene period, from which time there has been a decline to the generally accepted total of around 9,000 species living today. Though we know that the processes of evolution and extinction create equilibrium in nature, no caring ornithologist can fail to recognize that the increasing threats which birds are now facing can only accellerate the rate of extinction.

More land taken into use for housing, for industrial growth, for agriculture and for the extraction of natural resources means, inevitably, less land for birds; and at one level, this can be justified in terms of actual basic human survival. Not only is this at odds with those other threats that are typified by the dead Maltese swallow and the Exxon Valdez disaster; but ranged on the opposite side of the equation is the whole body of opinion that passionately values wildlife for what it is and for what it contributes to the soul of the human race.

Supporters of the view that everything is justifiable in terms of basic human survival have to contend with a rate of population increase that inevitably renders this basic human survival ever more difficult to achieve. Despite the scourge of AIDS, the increasing skill and social prominence of world health measures ensure that population increase is the single greatest threat to the birds of the world. The exponential nature of the increase is leading us to an unknown future, where natural habitat will be destroyed at an exponential rate merely to keep pace with sustaining this increased population. The environmental impact of this nightmare scenario will be incalculable, and leads us to the thought that we must surely be in the middle of one of the great extinction spasms of geological history.

In 1979 at Berkeley University, Luis Alvarez and three other physical scientists reached the conclusion that at the end of the Mesozoic era 66 million years ago the Earth was struck by a meteorite so great that it drastically changed the Earth's atmosphere and caused the mass extinction of substantial numbers of the species then living, dinosaurs included. Approximately 75,000 years ago there occurred in northern Sumatra a volcanic eruption so enormous that it has been calculated to have been one hundred times the magnitude of Krakatau. It blew out a phenomenal 1,000 cubic kilometers of solid material, and the effect on the Earth's atmosphere, and its living creatures, can only be imagined.

Simple statistical reasoning suggests that a meteor strike or a volcanic eruption of this magnitude is not only conceivable but also likely once every 10 or 100 million years. Indeed, mass extinction theories are based on such probabilities; but mass extinctions based on meteor strikes and volcanic eruptions are demonstrably beyond the scope of human interference. By contrast, what we are facing today is a mass extinction directly attributable to human interference, which in terms of both scientific theory and philosophical impact is a very different matter.

Professor E O Wilson of Harvard University, writing in the Summer 1988 issue of Orion, stated *There is an urgent need, greater I believe than the need to explore space, comparable to the exigencies of medical science, to prepare a map of biological diversity, especially in the tropical countries where the crisis is most severe. Time is running short to get this started.*

Harnessing endemism for survival.

BirdLife International (until 1993 known as the International Council for Bird Preservation, ICBP for short) is the leading international bird protection agency. They responded to Professor Wilson's call by publishing in 1992 a report entitled *Putting Biodiversity on the Map: priority areas for global conservation.* Until its publication there was insufficient quantified data on birds in the context of global biodiversity.

BirdLife International leads the world in the techniques for analysing information on bird distribution. Thus they are able to state catagorically that some 20% of all bird species are confined to just 2% of the earth's land surface. These are areas that also accommodate 70% of the world's threatened birds, as well as being of great importance for many other forms of life. From these data they conclude that adequate protection of the most critical areas for biodiversity would ensure the survival of a disproportionately wide variety of birds and other life forms. Conversely, the modification or destruction of habitat in these precious places would cause extinction on a massive scale.

Birds make the best indicators because they occur in most land habitats throughout the world, and are sensitive to environmental change. Their taxonomy and distribution are better known than those of any other reasonably large group of animals or plants. They disperse well and are better represented on islands. Birds are the only class of wildlife with all these attributes; but, as I have shown in this book, their appeal goes far beyond the merely objective and scientific. Their charisma is also directed to our emotions, and this is a powerful tool when motivating and arousing world opinion.

So far so good; but further work is needed to formulate a strategy. Using birds as indicators, Birdlife International gathered locality records for all species with breeding ranges of less than 50,000 square kilometers, about the size of Costa Rica or Denmark. By computerizing and mapping some 51,000 separate locality records, they concluded that there are 2,609 species or 27% of the world's birds with such small ranges.

In confirmation of many points which I have been at pains to emphasize, particularly the "Island Effect" and the quasi-island theory of "refuges", an analysis of bird distribution records shows that species with restricted ranges tend to occur together in places which are often islands or isolated patches of a particular habitat. BirdLife International have identified the boundaries of these natural groupings and have given to the areas so defined the name of Endemic Bird Areas (EBAs). There are 221 EBAs which embrace 2,484 species, a huge majority (95%) of all restricted-range birds. And by an odd quirk the number of both species and EBAs divide roughly equally between islands and continents.

By superimposing the EBA boundaries on a political map of the world it is easy to identify those countries with the greatest number of restricted-range birds; and, by asscociation, those with the greatest need for environmental protection or, at the very least, sustainable development of natural resources. Indonesia leads the way with 24 EBAs and 411 restricted-range species of which 339 are confined to the country. A further 7 countries (Mexico, Colombia, Ecuador, Brazil, Peru, the Philippines and Papua New Guinea) all have more than nine EBAs and over 100 restricted-range species.

This, then, is the basis of a sensible strategy to ensure that it can be possible to tread the minefield between the needs of the human world and the needs of the natural world. BirdLife International's painstaking accumulation and interpretation of data have provided a solid foundation from which it can be possible to mount a rescue operation. And within the exponentially growing world population there must be, by the law of averages, an exponentially growing number of people of resolve and goodwill to carry it out.

BirdLife International creates a new climate.

I opened this book with the thought that an increasing number of bird-watchers are travelling the world in search of ever more birds, and suggested that many of them might be motivated by the wish to increase their life lists. I also suggested that another approach might be to use these increased travel opportunities as a means of studying and attempting to understand the patterns of bird distribution.

By a somewhat circuitous route, on the way examining bird distribution, diversity and endemism, and sharing my personal response, I have tried to bring into the open a third and much needed objective for all travelling birdwatchers. Let me explain.

As we have seen, the strategic use of EBAs will focus the efforts of all people of goodwill onto the issue of environmental protection and the sustainable development of resources. I see this as a glimmer of optimism in the midst of the despair associated with worldwide habitat degradation.

On the other hand, there is always a tendency, when the issues seem too great to be resolved by the efforts of single individuals, for those single individuals to stand back and let "the others" do the work. But consider how the whole becomes greater than the sum of its parts when a large number of single individuals combine to achieve a common objective, making that objective easier to attain; in other words, the Mission Statement of the environmental lobby.

My prime purpose in visiting Hamilton, New Zealand in 1990 was to attend the World Conference of BirdLife International (then known as the International Council for Bird Preservation). As it turned out, I was present at a watershed moment in the history of Conservation; for it was at this conference that ICBP took the decision to join in partnership at nation level with the major bird protection organization of each nation. By turning the spotlight of each country's bird protection lobby outwards as well as inwards, and by raising the awareness of global protection issues by an order of magnitude, BirdLife immediately created a new climate in which their objectives could become easier to attain.

Envoi — go out and do it!

So I conclude with a positive invitation to all actual and potential travelling birdwatchers. Are you still interested in birdwatching around the world? Next year? Ten years hence?

Your answer must be a resounding YES! Here's what to do. Seek out these wonderful phenomena of diversity and endemism. Stand in a locality where you do not recognize a single bird! Work to the maxim — if you do not already do so — that "if we go for the endemics we'll pick up the rest on the way." Look for the Seven-coloured tanager, one of 11 species endemic to the forests of north-east Brazil; try Wallace's standardwing, a bird of paradise endemic to the Indonesian islands of Halmahera and Becan; and pause to think that each bird occurs nowhere else on earth.

Follow BirdLife International's advice. Go to Mount Kupe in the Cameroon Mountains EBA. Marvel (if you can find it) at its flagship bird, the Mount Kupe bush-shrike; but don't forget to eat the locally farmed mushrooms. And remember, as an eco-tourist, it is your very presence in the forest that is a major factor in ensuring its future.

Never was it easier to travel to watch birds. At random I have picked up a catalogue from a leading Bird Tour Company; their list of destinations is littered with countries high up in the EBA register. You will come back immeasurably more knowledgeable not only about the birds that you have seen, but also about the places where you have seen them. If you have been to an area with a high level of endemism you will now know what made it unique, as well as the principles behind its need for protection.

Talk about it — its wonders, its problems, its future, its very existence. Discuss it with friends, with other birdwatchers, with politicians, with industrialists, with anyone you like. Word travels fast, and soon other people will know about it, will begin to have some understanding — as you have — of the issues involved and the problems to be faced. This is one way to increase knowledge and create better informed public opinion; it is also a way to increase vitally important ecotourist revenues. Public opinion can move mountains and save rain forests from the chain saw, but in our entirely materialist world such efforts must be founded not on romanticised idealism but on the sound financial principles that eco-tourist revenues can provide.

If this is a sensible and practical way for birdwatchers to influence the major issues of worldwide environmental protection, sustainable development and eco-tourism, then we shall not have lived in vain and we shall have ensured that there are birds to watch in the future.

Reconciliation

In the prologue to this book I suggested that birdwatching is a hobby that is governed more by the heart than by the head. I went further and suggested a subtle but fundamental difference between the science of ornithology and the hobby of birdwatching; the former being subject to scientific processes and protocols, the latter being pursued as an end in itself and therefore likely to elicit a more personal and emotional response.

Here as elsewhere I have touched on the spiritual aspects of our response birds and other natural phenomena. In paying tribute to Charles Darwin's collossal contribution to the science of evolutionary biology, I have noted that his theories are now being interpreted in the light of contemporary thought and insights, citing as an example the concept of contingency.

Being spiritual animals, we find it hard to accept that evolutionary biology can be limited merely to the physics and chemistry of the life processes; that, in my earlier example, birds merely exist to pass their genes on to the next generation. We experience a vague unease that evolutionary biology is somehow an incomplete study of life, and in our efforts to achieve that completeness hold the view that if God — or the Plumed Serpent — did not exist it would be necessary to invent Him.

119

Evolutionary biology, Darwin's legacy, shows that we are at one with the animal kingdom; but if we accept that spirituality is a very real part of our make-up we must conclude that we have inherited it from our animal ancestors. Not only do we study the natural world, but we are constituent members of the natural world that we study. This must change for ever our view of conservation, and may even provide us with the meaning of life that we have all been so anxiously seeking.

BIBLIOGRAPHY

ATTENBOROUGH, David. Life on Earth. *Collins/BBC* 1979.

ATTENBOROUGH, David. The Living PLanet. *Collins/BBC* 1984.

ARDREY, Robert. African Genesis. 1993

AUSTIN, Oliver. Birds of the World. *Hamlyn Publishing Group.* 1961.

AXELL, Herbert and HOSKING, Eric. Minsmere; Portrait of a Bird Reserve. *Hutchinson of London.* 1977.

BIBBY, C.J. et al. Putting Biodiversity on the map: priority areas for global conservation. *"International Council for Bird Preservation".* 1992.

BOND, James. Birds of the West Indies. *Wm Collins.* 1936 (reprinted 1985).

BOND, James. Origin of the bird fauna of the West Indies. *Wilson Bulletin:60.* 1948.

BOWDEN, Liz. Where Spirits Meet. World Birdwatch 15:3 11-13. *"BirdLife International".* 1993.

BREWERS Dictionary of Phrase and Fable. *Cassell.* 1991 (14th Edition).

BUCKLEY, P.A. et al. (Eds.) Neotropical Ornithology. *AOU Ornithological Monographs No. 36.* 1985.

CAMPBELL, Bruce and LACK, Elizabeth (Eds.) A Dictionary of Birds. *British Ornithologists' Union/T. and A.D. Poyser.* 1985.

CARSON, Rachel. The Sea around us. *MacGibbon and Kee.* 1964.

CHAMBERS, Stuart. Birds of New Zealand; a locality guide. *Arun Books, Hamilton, New Zealand.* 1989.

CLEAVE, Andrew. Hummingbirds. *Hamlyn.* 1989.

COLBOURNE, R. The origin of the name KIWI. Notornis *(Journal of the Ornithological Society of New Zealand) 28:216.* 1981.

COLLAR, N J and ANDREW, P et al. Birds to watch, the ICBP World Checklist of Threatened Birds. *International Council for Bird Preservation.* 1988.

CRACRAFT, Joel. Continental Drift, Paleoclimatology and the Evolution and Biogeography of Birds. *J Zool Lond 169:455-545.* 1973.

CRACRAFT, Joel. Historical Biogeography and Patterns of Differentiation within the South American Avifauna; Areas of Endemism. *In BUCKLEY 1985, q.v.* 1985.

DARLING, Lois and Louis. Bird. *Methuen.* 1962.

DARWIN, Charles. On the Origin of Species. *London, John Murray.* 1859.

DOWNER, Audrey and SUTTON, Robert. Birds of Jamaica, a photographic field guide. 1990. *Cambridge University Press*. 1990.

ELLIOTT, Sir Hugh. *Island Populations*. In Birds of the World, Vol. IX, pp 2903-2905. Ed. John Gooders. *IPC Magazines*.

FALLA, R.A. et al. Collins guide to the birds of New Zealand. *Collins*. 1981 (reprinted 1987).

FLEGG, J J M and FRY, C Hilary et al. World Atlas of Birds. *Mitchell Beazley*. 1974.

FRANCIS, Peter. Volcanoes; a planetary perspective. *Clarendon Press*. 1993.

GREENWALT, C.H. Hummingbirds. *Doubleday and Co.* 1960.

GASTON, Kevin. Pers. comm. regarding Neotropical diversity. Department of Entomology, Natural History Museum, London.

GOULD, Stephen Jay. Wonderful Life: the Burgess Shale and the Nature of History. *Century Hutchinson*. 1989.

GOULD, Stephen Jay. Bully for Brontosaurus. *Century Hutchinson*

GRANT K A and GRANT V. Hummingbirds and their flowers. *Columbia University Press, New York*. 1968.

HABER, Harvey (Ed.) Insight Guide to Costa Rica. *APA Publications (HK) Ltd*. 1992.

HAFFER, Jurgen. Avian speciation in tropical South America. *Publ. Nuttall Orn. Club No. 14*. 1970.

HARDY, Alister. Darwin and the Spirit of Man. *Collins*. 1984.

HOWARD, Richard and MOORE, Alick. A complete checklist of birds of the world. *Academic Press*. 1991.

HOLLOM, P A D et al. Birds of the Middle East and North Africa. *T and A D Poyser Ltd*. 1988.

HOLM, Jessica. Field report on Kokakos in New Zealand. Broadcast by the BBC (Radio 4) Natural History Programme, 24.1.91. 1991.

JANZEN, Daniel H. (Ed.) Costa Rican Natural History. *University of Chicago Press*. 1983.

JOBLING, James A. A Dictionary of Scientific Bird Names. *Oxford University Press*. 1991.

JONSSON, Lars. Birds of Europe, with North Africa and the Middle East. *Christopher Helm/A & C Black*. 1992.

KING, Ben. Pers. comm. regarding suboscine passeriformes in S.E. Asia and Australia.

KINGDON, Jonathan. Island Africa. *Wm Collins.* 1990.

KRICHER, John H. A Neotropical companion. *Princeton University Press.* 1989/1990.

LACK, David. Island Biology, illustrated by the land birds of Jamaica. *Blackwell Scientific Publications.* 1976.

LINE, Les. Silence of the Songbirds. In National Geographic, Vol. 183, No. 6, pp 68-91. 1993.

LOFTIN, Horace and STEFFEE, Nina. A birder's field checklist to the Birds of Costa Rica. *Russ's Natural History Books* 1991.

MASLOW, Jonathan Evan. Bird of Life, Bird of Death. *Simon & Schuster/Viking.* 1986.

MATHEISSEN, Peter. The Snow Leopard. *Collins-Harvill* 1989.

MAYR, Ernst. Trends in avian systematics. Ibis 101: 293-302. 1959.

MAYR, Ernst. Animal species and evolution. Cambridge, MA: *Belknap Press, Harvard.* 1963.

MEARNS, Barbara and Richard. Biographies for Birdwatchers. *Academic Press.* 1988.

MOUNTFORD, Guy. Rare Birds of the World. *Wm Collins.* 1988.

PERRINS, Christopher M. et al. The illustrated Encyclopaedia of Birds; the definitive guide to Birds of the World. *Headline Book Publishing.* 1990.

PLATT, John. Department of Earth Sciences, Oxford University. Pers comm regarding a. Plate tectonics and the theories of Continental Drift; b. The collision zone between the Philippine Plate and the Australian-Indian Plate; and c. The study of paleo-biodiversity to show previous positions of Plates.

PUTTICK, John. The Haslemere Natural History Society, 1888-1988. The first Century. *Printed and published by the Committee of the Haslemere NHS.* 1988.

REDMAN, Nigel and HARRAP, Simon. Birdwatching in Britain; a site by site guide. *Christopher Helm.* 1987.

RIDGELEY, Robert S. and TUDOR, Guy. Birds of South America, Vol. I - The oscine passerines. *Oxford University Press.* 1987.

RICH, P.V. and RICH, T.H. The Central American dispersal route; biotic history and paleogeography. In Costa Rican Natural History, Ed. Janzen, q.v. 1983.

ROTHSCHILD, Miriam. Dear Lord Rothschild. *Balaban Publishers*. 1983.

SENNER, Stan. Frequent flyers - destination Neotropics. World Birdwatch, 15:3 7-8. *BirdLife International*. 1993.

SIBLEY, Charles G and AHLQUIST, Jon. Phylogeny and Classification of Birds; a Study in Molecular Evolution. *Yale University Press*. 1991.

SIBLEY, Charles G. and MONROE, Burt L. Distribution and Taxonomy of Birds of the World. *Yale University Press*. 1991.

SKINNER, Brian J and PORTER, Stephen C. The Dynamic Earth. *John Wiley and Sons*. 1989.

SKUTCH, Alexander F. The Imperative Call.

SKUTCH, Alexander F. A Naturalist amid Tropical Splendor. *University of Iowa Press*. 1987.

SKUTCH, Alexander F. and STILES, F. Gary. A guide to the birds of Costa Rica. *Cornell University Press*. 1989.

SNOW, David. The Cotingas. *Oxford University Press*. 1982.

SNOW, David. Pers. comm. regarding the South American suboscine passeriformes.

STILES, F. Gary. Introduction to the [Costa Rican] birds. In Costa Rican Natural History, *Ed. Janzen, q.v.* 1983.

TAYLOR, R H and THOMAS, B W. Eradication of Norway rats (Rattus norvegicus) from Hawea Island, Fiordland, using Brodifacoum. New Zealand Journal of Ecology, 12:23-32. 1989.

VEITCH, C R. Methods of Eradicating Feral Cats from Offshore Islands in New Zealand. Published in Conservation of Island Birds: Case studies for the management of threatened island species. *P J Moors ed. ICBP Technical Publication No. 3.* 1985.

WALLACE, Alfred Russel. Natural Selection and tropical nature. *London, Macmillan*. 1895.

WHITE, C.M.N and BRUCE, Murray D. 1986. The Birds of Wallacea. British Ornithologists Union Checklist No. 7.

WILLOCK, Colin. Kingdoms of the East. *Boxtree Press*. 1991.

WILSON, Edward O. The Diversity of Life. The Belknap Press of *Harvard University Press*. 1992.

WINDLEY, Brian F. The Evolving Continents. 2nd edition 1977. *John Wiley and Sons*. 1977.

WINTER, Tim and COLLYER, Graham. Around Haslemere and Hindhead in old photographs. *Alan Sutton Publishing, Stroud, Gloucestershire, England.* 1991.

YEKUTIEL, David. Personal communication regarding the contribution made by ornithology to the economy of Eilat, Israel.

CLASSIFIED LIST OF BIRD SPECIES MENTIONED IN THE TEXT

Based on "A complete checklist of birds of the world" second edition, 1991, by Richard Howard and Alick Moore. Published by Academic Press, London.

PROLOGUE

Hummingbird spp	Trochilidae
Resplendent quetzal	Pharomachrus mocinno
Tit spp	Paridae
Tanager spp	Thraupinae

Chapter 1 - In the beginning, a breath of fresh air

Great crested grebe	Podiceps cristatus
Red-backed shrike	Lanius collurio
Nightingale	Luscinia megarhynchos
Redstart	Phoenicurus phoenicurus

Chapter 2 - A chance encounter with a Dusky warbler

(Eurasian) Bittern	Botaurus stellaris
(White) spoonbill	Platalea leucorodia
Gadwall	Anas streptera
Goosander	Mergus merganser
Smew	Mergus albellus
Marsh harrier	Circus aeruginosus
(Pied) avocet	Recurvirostra avosetta
Little ringed plover	Charadrius dubius
Black-tailed godwit	Limosa limosa
(Ruddy) turnstone	Arenaria interpres
(Eurasian) woodcock	Scolopax rusticola
(Red) knot	Calidris canutus
Sanderling	Calidris alba
Curlew sandpiper	Calidris ferruginea
Little tern	Sterna albifrons
Razorbill	Alca torda
Guillemot	Uria aalge
Black guillemot	Cepphus grylle
(Atlantic) puffin	Fratercula arctica
(European) nightjar	Caprimulgus europaeus
(River) kingfisher	Alcedo atthis
Great spotted woodpecker	Picoides major

Dipper	Cinclus cinclus
Nightingale	Luscinia megarhynchos
Bluethroat	Luscinia svecicus
Redstart	Phoenicurus phoenicurus
Bearded reedling	Panurus biarmicus
Zitting cisticola	Cisticola juncidis
Wood warbler	Phylloscopus sibilatrix
Dusky warbler	Phylloscopus fuscatus
Spotted flycatcher	Muscicapa striata
Pied flycatcher	Ficedula hypoleuca
Long-tailed tit	Aegithalos caudatus

Chapter 3 - The dead swallow and the Hoopoe lark

Hoopoe	Upupa epops
Hoopoe lark	Alaemon alaudipes
(Barn) swallow	Hirundo rustica
(Northern) wheatear	Oenanthe oenanthe
Black-eared wheatear	Oenanthe hispanica
Pygmy nuthatch	Sitta pygmaea
Brown-headed nuthatch	Sitta pusilla
Red-breasted nuthatch	Sitta canadensis
White-breasted nuthatch	Sitta carolinensis

Chapter 4 - Farming the forest for the future

Bannerman's turaco	Tauraco bannermani
Resplendent quetzal	Pharomachrus mocinno
Hoopoe lark	Alaemon alaudipes
(Barn) swallow	Hirundo rustica
Mount Kupe bush-shrike	Malaconotus kupeensis
Grey-necked picathartes	Picathartes oreas

Chapter 5 - Two sides of one coin

Ostrich	Struthio camelus
Rhea spp	Rhea spp
Cassowary spp	Casuarius spp
Emu	Dromaius novaehollandiae
Brown kiwi	Apteryx australis
Little spotted kiwi	Apteryx owenii
Great spotted kiwi	Apteryx haastii
Little blue penguin	Eudyptula minor
Cook's petrel	Pterodroma cookii
Flesh-footed shearwater	Puffinus carneipes
Fluttering shearwater	Puffinus gavia
Buller's shearwater	Puffinus bulleri

Kaka	Nestor meridionalis
Yellow-billed parrot	Amazona collaria
Boobook owl (Morepork)	Ninox novaeseelandiae
Red-billed streamertail	Trochilus polytmus
Black-billed streamertail	Trochilus scitulus
Ochre-bellied flycatcher	Mionectes oleagineus
Short-tailed pygmy-tyrant	Myiornis ecaudatus
Common tody-flycatcher	Todirostrum cinereum
Royal flycatcher	Onychorhynchus coronatus
Sad flycatcher	Myiarchus barbirostris
Rufous-tailed flycatcher	Myiarchus validus
Scissor-tailed flycatcher	Tyrannus forficata
Redwing	Turdus iliacus
Kinglet spp	Regulus spp
New Zealand grey warbler	Gerygone igata
Long-tailed tit	Aegithalos caudatus
Penduline tit	Remiz pendulinus
Stitchbird	Notiomystis cincta
New Zealanmd bellbird	Anthornis melanura
Tui	Prosthemadura novaeseelandiae
Yellow-shouldered grassquit	Loxipasser anoxanthus
Orangequit	Euneornis campestris
Northern oriole	Icterus galbula
Oropendola spp	Psaracolius spp
Jamaican blackbird	Nesopsar nigerrimus
(Eurasian) goldfinch	Carduelis carduelis
Weaver spp	Ploceus spp
Kokako	Callaeas cinerea

Chapter 7 - Of Rafts and Ratites

Ostrich	Struthio camelus
Rhea spp	Rhea spp
Cassowary spp	Casuarius spp
Emu	Dromaius novaehollandiae
Penguin spp	Spheniscidae
New Zealand brown teal	Anas aucklandica
New Zealand falcon	Falco novaezeelandiae
American purple gallinule	Gallinula martinica
Hummingbird spp	Trochilidae
Bee hummingbird	Calypte helenae
Trogon spp	Trogonidae
Barbet spp	Capitonidae
Sad flycatcher	Myiarchus barbirostris
Olivaceous flycatcher	Myiarchus tuberculifer

Rifleman	Acanthisitta chloris
Skylark	Alauda arvensis
(European) robin	Erythacus rubecula
Nightingale	Luscinia megarhynchos
Stitchbird	Notiomystis cinctus
New Zealand bellbird	Anthornis melanura
Tui	Prosthemadura novaeseelandiae
Kokako	Callaeas cinerea
Saddleback	Creadion carunculatus

Chapter 8 - A Fabled Eldorado

King penguin	Aptenodytes patagonicus
Emperor penguin	Aptenodytes forsteri
Semicollared hawk	Accipiter collaris
Ornate hawk-eagle	Spizaetus ornatus
Collared forest falcon	Micrastur semitorquatus
Pigeon spp	Columbidae
Macaw spp	Ara spp
Cuckoo spp	Cuculidae
Lesser ground-cuckoo	Morococcyx erythropygus
White-tipped sicklebill	Eutoxeres aquila
Hermit spp	Phaethornis spp et al
Andean hillstar	Oreotrochilus estella
Elegant trogon	Trogon elegans
Tody spp	Todus spp
Turquoise-browed motmot	Eumomota superciliosa
Collared aracari	Pteroglossus torquatus
Fiery-billed aracari	Pteroglossus frantzii
Woodpecker spp	Picidae
Lesser-spotted woodpecker	Picoides minor
Great spotted woodpecker	Picoides major
Hairy woodpecker	Picoides villosus
Andean flicker	Colaptes rupicola
Woodcreeper spp	Dendrocolaptidae
Foliage-gleaner spp	Phylidor/Automolus spp
Antbird spp	Formicariidae
Western wood pewee	Contopus sordidulus
Silky-flycatcher	Ptilogonys phainoptila
Riverside wren	Thryothorus semibadius
Bay wren	Thryothorus nigricapillus
(Winter) wren	Troglodytes troglodytes
Bahama mockingbird	Mimus grundlachii
Nightingale-thrush spp	Catharus spp
Chiguanco thrush	Turdus chiguanco

Tanager spp	Thraupinae
Elfin woods warbler	Dendroica angelae
Redstart spp	Myioborus spp

Chapter 9 - Kokako song

Boobook owl (Morepork)	Ninox novaeseelandiae
Blackbird	Turdus merula
Chaffinch	Fringilla coelebs
Kokako	Callaeas cinerea

Chapter 10 - Just Deserts

Brown kiwi	Apteryx australis
Emperor penguin	Aptenodytes forsteri
Greater roadrunner	Geococcyx californianus
Lesser roadrunner	Geococcyx velox
Ceylon frogmouth	Batrachostomus moniliger
Eye-ringed flatbill	Rhynchocyclus brevirostris
Phainopepla	Phainopepla nitens
White-crowned black wheatear	Oenanthe leucopyga
Hooded wheatear	Oenanthe monacha
Black wheatear	Oenanthe luecura
Northern wheatear	Oenanthe oenanthe
Mourning wheatear	Oenanthe lugens
Black-eared wheatear	Oenanthe hispanica
Desert wheatear	Oenanthe deserti
Isabelline wheatear	Oenanthe isabellina
Blackstart	Cercomela melanura
Palestine sunbird	Nectarinia osea
Black-throated sparrow	Amphispiza bilineata
Tristram's (Syrian) serin	Serinus syriacus
Trumpeter finch	Rhodopechys githaginea
Sinai rosefinch	Carpodacus synoicus
House sparrow	Passer domesticus
(Eurasian) tree sparrow	Passer montanus

Chapter 11 - Streamertails at breakfast

Kiwi spp	Apteryx spp
Bristle-thighed curlew	Numenius tahitiensis
(Eurasian) woodcock	Scolopax rusticola
(Eurasian) Tawny owl	Strix aluco
Common potoo	Nyctibius griseus
(European) nightjar	Caprimulgus europeaus
Coquette spp	Lophornis spp
Red-billed streamertail	Trochilus polytmus

Trainbearer	*Lesbia spp*
Anna's hummingbird	*Calypte anna*
Sad flycatcher	*Myiarchus barbirostris*
Blackbird	*Turdus merula*
White-chinned thrush	*Turdus aurantius*
White-eyed thrush	*Turdus jamaicensis*
American robin	*Turdus migratorius*
Blackcap	*Sylvia atricapilla*
Black-throated blue warbler	*Dendroica caerulescens*
American redstart	*Setophaga ruticilla*

Chapter 12 - Meeting the Plumed Serpent

Red jungle fowl	*Gallus gallus*
Resplendent quetzal	*Pharomachrus mocinno*
Andean hillstar	*Oreotrochilus estella*
Bare-necked umbrellabird	*Cephalopterus glabricollis*
Wallace's standardwing	*Semioptera wallacei*

Epilogue - Farewell and hail

Osprey	*Pandion haliaetus*
Vervain hummingbird	*Mellisuga minima*
Mount Kupe bush-shrike	*Malaconotus kupeensis*
Musician wren	*Cyphorinus ardus*
Nightingale	*Luscinia megarhynchos*
New Zealanmd bellbird	*Anthornis melanura*
Seven-cloured tanager	*Tangara fastuosa*
(Western) greenfinch	*Carduelis chloris*
Wallace's standardwing	*Semioptera wallacei*
Blue bird of paradise	*Paradisaea rudolphi*
Raven	*Corvus corax*

GLOSSARY

A

ACCLIMATIZATION SOCIETIES. Societies charged in the 19th Centuray with attracting new settlers to the British colonies, and with making them feel at home. Responsible for translocating familiar British birds to New Zealand as part of this process.

ADAPTIVE RADIATION. Divergence in the characters of related species that enables them to exploit different kinds of opportunity, usually ecological.

ADAPTATION. Evolutionary process whereby species change to suit a changed set of circumstances. Process usually starts with behaviour which leads to anatomical and morphological change, and eventually to genetic change.

AEPYORNIS. The extinct Elephant bird of Madagascar. Gave rise to the legend of the Roc.

AFROTROPICAL REGION. Essentially Africa south of the Sahara, excluding Madagascar and the Comoro Islands, but including Zanzibar, Pemba, Mafia and the Gulf of Guinea.

ANATOMY. The science of bodily structure.

ANDESITE. A volcanic rock found in the Andes, and elsewhere.

ARAWAK. Peace-loving pre-Columbian aborigine peoples living in the Caribbean and Central America, driven to the edge of extinction by the warlike Caribs, a process completed by Europeans.

ASTHENOSPHERE. Plastic zone within the earth's mantle, 350 to 100 kms deep, where the balance between temperature and pressure ensures that the rocks have little strength.

AUSTRALASIAN REGION. Faunal region comprising Australia, New Guinea, and New Zealand and its dependencies. The Lesser Sundas are more problematical. See also Oriental Region, Wallacea, Wallace's Line and Weber's Line.

B

BIODIVERSITY. The total variety of life on earth. By extension, the total variety within a group of life forms, eg birds.

BIOGEOGRAPHY. The study of the geographical distribution of living things.

BIRD RACE. A form of twitching (qv) in which teams compete to see how many species they can see in a set time. Useful device for raising funds for conservation.

BROMELIAD. Plants of the Neotropical family Bromeliaceae, mainly epiphytic (qv) and able to withstand drought.

BUSHMEAT. Wild creatures hunted for food in (usually African) forests.

C

CASH CROPS. Crops grown for sale, as opposed to consumption by the grower. A means of earning foreign exchange.

COLLISION ZONE. Where two tectonic plates collide to create mountain ranges, eg Alps, Himalayas. See also Convergent margins.

CONGENER. Member of the same genus as another species, as in "The Sad flycatcher (Myiarchus barbirostris) is different from its mainland congener, the Olivaceous flycatcher (M. tuberculifer.)" The adjective is "congeneric."

COMPETITION. Interaction between two or more individuals, of the same or different species, for a resource (eg food or nest sites) that is in short supply.

CONSERVATION. Preservation of environmental entrigrity. A process of balancing the needs of nature with those of humans.

CONTINENTAL CRUST. That part of the earth's crust on which continents are being rafted around by the action of plate tectonics.

CONTINENTAL DIVIDE. Mountain range (usually), that divides a landmass along a watershed.

CONTINENTAL DRIFT. The theory that continents have drifted to their present positions as a result of Plate Tectonics.

CONTINGENCY. The process whereby one activity happens as a direct result of another. Implicit randomness.

CONTINGENT ADAPTIVE PRESSURE. The theory that adds the concept of contingeny (qv) to that of Natural Selection (qv); the implication that the conditions which impose adaptive pressure on species arose by chance.

CONVERGENT MARGINS. Where 2 tectonic plates move towards each other. See also Subduction zone, Collision zone and Volcanic arc.

COQUETTE. A genus (Lophornis) of hummingbirds, distributed from southwest Mexico to central Bolivia and southeast Brazil.

CORDILLERA. Spanish word for mountain range.

D

DIVERSITY. See Biodiversity.

DNA. The basic genetic material of all life forms. It is possible, by the process known as DNA-DNA hybridization, to determine degrees of genetic similarity between pairs of species, from which a taxonomy can be established. This is still (1993) a controversial theory, and many authorities do not consider it sufficiently proven to warrant its use as a replacement for older classifications based on anatomy and morphology.

DROMORNIS. Extinct flightless bird from Australia.

E

ECOLOGY. The study of living creatures in relation to their environment.

ECOLOGICAL NICHE. The particular, and often small, part of the environment to which specialist creatures have adapted.

ECOSYSTEM. The sum of all factors that make up a particular environment.

ECO-TOURISM. The particular form of tourism where participants take an interest in wildlife to the extent of paying for a wildlife experience, of having a particular focus for wildlife study, and of encouraging the wise and sustainable use of the environment that makes their objectives possible.

ELAENIA. Sub-division of Tyrant-flycatchers.

ELFINWOOD. The forest zone at the highest altitude on tropical mountains, characterized by vegetation that is twisted and stunted in response to increased moisture and decreased sunlight.

ENDEMISM/ENDEMIC. Term applied to a species, genus etc meaning that it is restricted to a stated area. Analogous with "Restricted range" which BirdLife International interpret as 50,000 square kilometers. See also RESTRICTED-RANGE BIRDS.

ENDEMIC BIRD AREA (EBA) An area, indicated by an analysis of distribution records, where there is a concentration of endemic bird species.

EPIPHYTE. A plant able to subsist in and take nourishment from the air. See Bromeliad.

F

FAUNAL REGIONS. A system, propounded in the 19th Century by Dr P L Sclater and Alfred Russel Wallace and now accepted worldwide, that divides the world and its fauna and flora into six zoogeographical areas.

FLAGSHIP SPECIES. Prominent species that can be used to focus public attention for the purposes of conservation, political or marketing strategy.

FLATBILL. A sub-division of the Tyrant-flycatchers.

FLIGHTLESSNESS. A condition found in all ratites and some other species (eg rails and cormorants) resulting from the "island effect."

FOULNESS. A coastal area on the north shore of the Thames Estuary, where plans to build an airport were dropped partly as a result of conservation pressure.

FOUNDER EFFECT. A term used in evolutionary biology. When colonists from a species/population arrive in a new location or island they may take with them a genetic inheritance that relates to the parent species/population either differently or only partially.

FURNARIOIDEA. The assemblage of sub-oscine passerines that contains the woodcreepers, ovenbirds, antbirds and their allies.

G

G7 GROUPING. The seven leading industrial nations - USA, UK, France, Germany, Canada, Japan and Italy. (Check accuracy please!!!!)

GEOCOCCYX. Genus of ground-cuckoo containing the two Roadrunner species.

GEOPHYSICS. The science that studies the physics of the earth.

134

GIGANTISM. A condition, akin to flightlessness, that results from the "island effect" and renders species larger than would be expected by comparison with congeners and other similar species.

GONDWANALAND. The name given to the southern part of Pangaea (qv) that broke away and fragmented to form Australia, New Zealand, South America, Antarctica, Africa and India. Named after a rock type found in India.

GREATER ANTILLES. The islands of Jamaica, Cuba, Hispaniola (Haiti and Dominican Republic) and Puerto Rico. See also Todies.

GUANACASTE. The arid north-western province of Costa Rica, generally the most southerly point reached by some bird species from further north that are adapted to such conditions.

H

HELICONIA. Plants of the family Helicaniaceae, having huge elon-gate paddle-shaped leaves, and dis-tinctive red, orange or yellow bracts, reminiscent of the shape of lobster claws, that surround and protect the smaller flowers. Attractive to hummingbird pollina-tors. See Parallel evolution.

HUMBOLDT CURRENT. Cold cur-rent flowing north up the west coast of South America.

HYLAEA. Greek word for "forest" applied by Alexander von Humboldt to the tropical rain for-est.

I

ICE AGE. Pleistocene glaciation.

INTERCHANGE OF SPECIES. Process, most apparent in Central America and parts of Indonesia, whereby species are exchanged between large continental land-masses.

ISOLATING MECHANISM. Unique process whereby each species retains its individual integrity; eg plumage recognition, courtship rituals, niche preference, pollination mechanisms etc.

ISOLATION. A mechanism in the process of speciation that tends to prevent cross-mating between species and populations of species; eg as a result of mountain uprise or when islands are colonized.

J

JUNGLE. A term properly only applied to disturbed secondary growth forest.

K

KAKA. Forest parrot endemic to North Island, New Zealand.

KINGBIRD. Sub-division of Tyrant-flycatchers.

KINGLET. Widely distributed birds of the genus Regulus. American ter-minology.

L

LANDBRIDGE. Any topographical feature linking landmasses. Can be formed from arcs of volcanic islands (eg Central America) or by lowered sea levels during periods of glaciation (eg Bering Straits).

LAURASIA. Name given to the northern part of Pangaea (qv). Composite word from "Laurentia", the old name for the pre-Cambrian core of Canada, and "Eurasia".

LESSER SUNDAS. Chain of islands in Indonesia from Bali in the west to Timor in the East. Of volcanic origin.

LIFEBOAT ISLANDS. Term used in New Zealand to denote offshore islands that have been cleared of introduced predators prior to the translocation of endangered endemic birds, eg Little Barrier Island.

LITHOSPHERE. The top 100 kms of the earth's structure incorporating the uppermost part of the mantle and all of the crust. Literally "rock sphere".

M

MAGMA. Molten rock.

MARGINS. Edges of tectonic plates where they come into contact with other plates and cause a variety of geophysical conditions.

MARINE CONTOURS. Lines joining points of similar depth in the sea, synonymous to isobaths.

MARSUPIAL. Order of mammals whose young are born in a very imperfect state (see Neonate) and are carried in a pouch by the female. See also Placenta.

MESOSPHERE. Zone within the earth, at depths between 2,883 and 350 kms, where temperature and pressure are in equilibrium allowing iron to exhibit great strength and great temperature.

MICROCLIMATE. Climatic conditions restricted to small areas usually by topography.

MOA. Extinct ratites from New Zealand.

MONTANE FOREST. Cool, moist mountain ecosystem, in altitude below cloud forest.

MORPHOLOGY. The science of form and shape.

N

NATURAL SELECTION. Theory, published by Charles Darwin in "On the Origin of Species", that it is the physical and biological environment of each species that imposes the conditions under which it must adapt to survive. See also Contingent adaptive pressure.

NEONATE. Imperfectly formed young of a marsupial mammal, carried in the pouch by the female.

NEOTROPICS. Faunal region extending from the northern edge of the tropical rain forest in Mexico (approx 20 degrees N) south to Cape Horn (approx 57 degrees south), together with the West Indies and other islands near South America.

NOMENCLATURE. The scientific naming of species and subspecies and of the other categories (eg genera, families etc) in which species may be classified. See also Taxonomy.

O

OCEANIC CRUST. That part of the earth's crust under the oceans that is spreading apart as a result of spreading centres (qv).

ORIENTAL REGION. The mainly tropical region of southern and southeast Asia; from the Hindu Kush in the North and the Indus Valley in the west, eastward to the East China Sea at approx 30 degrees north and southward to include the Greater Sundas, Borneo, Sulawesi and the Philippines. The Lesser Sundas are more problematic. See also Wallacea, Wallace's Line, Weber's Line and Australasian Region.

OSCINE. Sub-division of the order Passeriformes, usually considered more advanced, and possessing a developed syringeal musculature (qv) capable of producing true song. (See Sub-oscines.)

P

PAIRS OF SPECIES. Phenomenon generated when a mountain range (or other topographical feature) arises in such a way as to isolate two populations of a species to the point where separate speciation occurs. Particularly clearly demonstrated in southern Costa Rica where pairs of wrens, aracaris, manakins and cotingas exist one on each side of the Cordillera de Talamanca. See also Superspecies.

PANGAEA. The ancient super-continent prior to its fragmentation into Gondwanaland (South) and Laurasia (North).

PARALLEL EVOLUTION. An evolutionary process whereby two separate but dependent life forms develop to the point of mutual service; eg hummingbirds with curved bills that allow them exclusive access to flowers with curved corollas, eg Heliconias.

PARAMO. Tropical alpine shrubland in the mountains of western Central and South America, south from southern Costa Rica to the equator.

PASSERINES. The order Passeriformes, more generally known as the perching birds, and comprising roughly 60% of all known birds.

PEWEE. Sub-division of tyrant-flycatchers.

PHOEBE. Sub-division of tyrant-flycatchers.

PLACENTA. The structure that unites the unborn mammal to the womb of its mother and establishes the nutritive connection. See also Marsupial.

PLATE TECTONICS. Theory based on the earth's internal convection, which permits plates of the lithosphere (qv) to slide sideways.

PODOCARP. Eastern and southern genus of trees in the yew family. Common in New Zealand.

POPULATION. A biological term to denote any group of organisms belonging to the same species at the same time and place.

PUNA. Tropical alpine grassland in the Andes south from the equator to Peru and Bolivia.

R

RAIN SHADOW EFFECT. Condition prevailing on the lee-ward side of a mountain range whereby arid conditions prevail.

RATITES. Group of flightless birds (Ostrich, Rhea, Emu, Cassowary, Kiwi and several extinct species) which, having no need for flight muscles, lack a deeply keeled breast bone. From the Latin word "ratus", a raft.

REFUGES. Fragmented areas of rain forest left behind in areas of savannah that are expanding due to the dessicating effect of glaciation. An example of circumstances that induce speciation and endemism.

RESTRICTED-RANGE BIRDS. Birds restricted in range to a maximum of 50,000 square kilometers. See also Endemism.

S

SAHUL SHELF. The continental shelf on which lie Australia and New Guinea; the eastern boundary of Wallacea (qv) and roughly contiguous to Weber's line (qv).

SAVANNAH. Grassland ecosystem, scattered with trees and shrubs.

SEDENTARY. Non-migratory.

SPECIATION. The process whereby new species evolve.

SPREADING CENTRES. Fractures in the lithosphere where two tectonic plates move apart. Clearly demonstrated in widening of the Atlantic Ocean and marked by the mid-Atlantic ridge. Also known as Divergent Margins. See also Oceanic crust.

SUBDUCTION ZONE. Where one tectonic plate slides beneath another, giving rise to vulcanism and the formation of volcanic arcs. See also Convergent margins.

SUB-OSCINES. Sub-division of the order Passeriformes, usually considered more primitive, and possessing an underdeveloped syringeal musculature (qv) incapable of true song. (See Oscines.)

SUBSPECIES. Defined by Ernst Mayr as "geographically defined aggregates of local populations which differ taxonomically from other such subdivisions of a species." Population which can be distinguished morphologically from other populations of the same species. Synonymous with the term "race."

SUNDA SHELF. The Continental shelf on which lies southeast Asia. The western boundary of Wallacea (qv) and roughly contiguous to Wallace's line (qv).

SUPER-SPECIES. A term introduced by Ernst Mayr to denote a grouping of species, of lesser rank than a sub-genus, and having no status within the nomenclature; a group of single evolutionary ancestry and of very closely related species with a mutually exclusive geographic distribution. See also Pairs of species and Todies.

SUSTAINABLE DEVELOPMENT. Management strategy whereby economic and agricultural practices retain environmental integrity. Examples include the marketing of honey from Kilum Mountain, Cameroon, to the economic benefit of local people; and eco-tourism that relies on the good state of the environment and its wildlife.

SYRINGEAL MUSCULATURE. The muscles that control the syrinx or organ of voice and song. See also Oscines and Sub-oscines.

T

TAXONOMY. The science of classification. Originally based on criteria of anatomy and morphology, which some authorities still consider to be the most accurate. Increasing use of DNA-based criteria, awaiting general acceptance.

THYLACINE. The marsupial wolf.

TODIES. Single genus (Todus) of Coraciiform birds, uniquely restricted to the Greater Antilles (qv). Considered by some to be a Super species (qv). Individual species endemic to Jamaica, Cuba and Puerto Rico. Two species endemic to Hispaniola and separated altitudinally.

TOPOGRAPHY. A description of all surface features, both natural and artificial, of a particular region.

TWITCHING. A branch of bird-watching concerned with rarities and vagrants.

TYRANNOIDEA. The assemblage of sub-oscine passerines that includes cotingas, manakins, tyrant-flycatchers and their allies.

TYRANNULET. Sub-division of tyrant-flycatchers.

TYSTIE. Dialect word for the Black guillemot, from Orkneys and Shetlands.

V

VAGRANT. A bird wandering outside the normal migration range.

VOLCANIC ARC. Series of volcanoes parallel to but about 150 kms from a convergent plate margin (qv) and its resultant subduction zone (qv).

W

WADI. Arabic word for seasonally dried-up water course.

WALLACEA. The area in Indonesia, between Wallace's Line (qv) and Weber's Line (qv) where the interchange of species between the Oriental and Australasian realms is most marked.

WALLACE'S LINE. Line postulated by Alfred Russel Wallace and roughly contiguous with the Sunda Shelf (qv) that marks the faunal change between species of Oriental origin and those of Australasian origin. Runs between Bali and Lombok, Borneo and Sulawesi and south of the Philippines. See also Wallacea.

WEBER'S LINE. Line postulated in 1902 to show the position of a more accurate faunal balance than that acknowledged by Wallace's line (qv) between Oriental and Australasian faunas. Roughly contiguous with Sahul shelf (qv).

INDEX

C

D

E

H

I

J

N

O

P

British Trust for Ornithology

BUCKINGHAMSH

BUCKS BIRD CL

SATURDAY 12th NOVEMBER 1994 M

"MIG

The conference is open to ANYONE
other enthusiasts and learn more a
behaviour.

The day will commence at 9.30am
coffee, and an opportunity to view
competitions and the raffle. Lectu
continue, with a short break, unti
chance to look around before more
conference will end at 4.45 - 5.0C

SPEAKERS and TOPICS are :-   1)
Ray Waters, BTO - Britain's Role
Chris Mead, BTO - Looking Over Th
David Glue, BOU - Birds and Weath
John Bowler, WWT - Bewick's Swans
                                2)
Peter Edwards, Hughendon RG - Rin
                               W
Graeme Taylor, Bucks BC - Comings
Rob Young, Herts County Recorder

Apart from the BTO and Bucks Bi
commercial STALLS and DISPLAYS by

COST (including coffee, tea and a
    £12 per person; £20 per couple
    (Refunds available for cancellat
- minus 20% administration fee)
TICKETS MUST be PRE-BOOKED from
Lane, Wendover, Aylesbury, Bucks

RE BIRD CLUB

Reg. Charity no. 802292

BTO CONFERENCE

RIAL HALL, MANOR ROAD, WENDOVER

TION"

d will provide an opportunity to meet
t a fascinating aspect of bird

h the registration of participants,
e stalls and displays and enter the
will commence at 10.30am and
unch. This will present a further
ks, separated by afternoon tea. The

g talks :-
he East Atlantic Flyway
e - 20 years on Steps Hill

om Slimbridge to Russia
t talks :-
on the Chiltern Escarpment at
gton
Goings - Bucks ringing recoveries
ration at Tring Reservoirs - The
est Herts Flyway ?!

ub there will be a variety of
l bird and conservation groups.

lunch)
0 for student / over 65
up to 7 days prior to the conference

Taylor, Field House, 54 Halton
AU   Tel. 0296 625796

ach -